CHANGING TIMES

Memoirs of a Young Seaman
1946–1951

T. James (Jim) Bailey

Pen Press

First published in Great Britain by Pen Press

All paper used in the printing of this book has been made from
wood grown in managed, sustainable forests.

ISBN 978-1-906710-99-6

Printed and bound in the UK
Pen Press is an imprint of Indepenpress Publishing Limited
25 Eastern Place
Brighton
BN2 1GJ

A catalogue record of this book is available from
the British Library

Cover design Enid Bailey

Dedicated to my wife Enid,
who has sailed with me at all times
through rough and calm seas.

To Paulette.

Happy reading and
Keep dancing

Jim Barry

*A map of the main Brazilian ports I visited,
including the magnificent River Amazon.*

Acknowledgements

I could not have reached this far, without the encouragement of Enid my wife, who has to a large extent seen me through my teething troubles with the computer and my lack of accepted grammar.

To be honest I hadn't really appreciated the amount of work and effort that has to be put into such an enterprise. Whether or not this epistle will ever go beyond our front door is another matter. We will have to see!!

The other person who has played an important part in helping to rationalize my writing, is Brian Holdsworth, for his help collating everything together in some sort of order. I certainly had never realized how much I owed to the wonderful world of the computer.

To both Enid and Brian I am most indebted but any remaining mistakes either factual or grammatical are entirely mine.

And to all those characters I met during the period of this book, without whom it wouldn't have been such wonderful memories.

Some of the photographs have been obtained from the Internet or books and I acknowledge the owners of the copyright.

Contents

Continued…

Foreword

I felt cold, miserable, and I really don't know how else to explain my feelings. Oh yes of course extremely lonely. Not without reason, for I am on board the S.S. *Lalande*, a merchant ship in my capacity as a junior cadet in the Irish Sea. Two weeks previously I had been lucky enough to go north about to Glasgow and thence to Liverpool in relatively calm seas but now well down with cargo and a gale in progress it is not good news. Never again, I say to myself, as the ship rolls in a heavy sea and gale force winds pound on the deck. I must say it was then that I had my doubts as to my choice of career.

Why anybody, let alone myself should decide to attempt to write a book about my early life beats me. It was however a fascinating time, with the war not long finished and the world trying to pick up the threads once again. I suppose if you feel that you have something to impart, then the obvious thing to do, is to have a go and attempt to put it down on paper.

In my case it was the chance to go to sea as a young officer, with a famous old shipping company Lamport & Holt Line, which would give me a wonderful start. But not without a lot of hard graft and a lot of studying if I was to get anywhere.

I have always been fascinated by folk all my life and stories of the past have held me spellbound. Of course the early days in my life time will not be the same for others, unless we happen to be the same generation. I suppose what I am trying to say rather badly, is that every generation has something to say and this is my interpretation of my youth.

One memory that stands out from my childhood is building a canoe with my father which I called 'Ratty'. This was a name that had evolved from my constant reading of that wonderful book *Wind in the Willows* by Kenneth Graham.

Ratty is launched

Before the war Loughborough Boat Club was at the centre of our lives. As war broke out everything was shelved but Mr Barsnel, an old boy who was a boat builder on Derby Road, continued his craft. I spent many happy hours with him and it was here that the inspiration came to build my first boat. Who would have thought that about 25 years later I would again build a boat, this time a catamaran *Determination* and sail it single-handed across the Atlantic.

Chapter 1

Early days

It is only fair to acquaint the reader with my own situation. Unfortunately due to bad health my education was very spasmodic, to the point that my parents were desperate as to the lack of my academic progress. I had a series of schools which I attended, one was the local primary school then a series of one-to-one local teachers, where I fared no better, as my attendance was so irregular.

Eventually, I was lucky enough to go to Lougborough Grammar School, the school I attended for my secondary education and I think they did their best. All the male Baileys had attended but as my attendance was spasmodic, I think the school were very kind to put up with me. I resided at the bottom of the class, but as was kindly said by our form master, Mr Foxon when I reached the third form, and maintained a steady 31st place "Everything needs good foundations, Bailey, and you seem to fit the bill."

To be fair to myself I had acute asthma and the advances in cure or prevention were very far away. I was forever off school to the extent and to the horror of my parents the school's inspector turned up one day for an explanation. So there you are!

Anyway 1945 loomed up and it was then that a possible career, or job on a farm might be a solution or at least a start. This was discussed at great length, by Dad and his brother Don, who was a farmer at Nanpantan, just outside Loughborough. As far as I can remember, not being paid of course, I was able to ascertain on his farm if this was the sort of life that well might do for me.

Unknown to me however, Dad and Uncle Don, had taken it upon themselves, not an unusual procedure in the Bailey family, that having decided that if I was to get on at all in my willingness to have a go that I should go away and live in.

The two of them looked around for some family farm that hopefully might instil into me the desire to have such a career. So it was in early summer of 1946 that my parents took me to a Shropshire farm. I have to say that the experience I was to have along with another young hopeful, whose name I have long forgotten and this also applies to the farmer. I am sure the old saying 'that you only remember the good things that happen to you' is very true, I do remember the farm however which was in sight of the Wrekin a well known hill in that vicinity.

What I will never forget is the awful conditions we two lads found ourselves in. Had my parents remained at the farm long enough to have a good look round, it is doubtful if they would have allowed me to stay. On reflection I think the farmer couldn't get rid of them quickly enough. It was soon obvious to my new friend and I that we were there to do as required, as we soon found out. The farmer turned out to be a hard task master. We met his wife and followed her to the attic where we both had to sleep, a small room with a low ceiling, bare floor boards, no curtains at the window and the only light was half way down the stairs. The next few days, indeed the rest of the time we were there, confirmed all we wished to know and that was quite simply we were forced labour from morning to night. One morning, I was cleaning out a stable block, when I heard a noise on the other side of the yard then a scream. Downing tools, I rushed out to see the farmer laying into my friend with the whip he always carried and was using with great force.

That night in our attic we vowed to get away, but we had no access to a phone and we were some miles from a village. Suffice it to say we eventually, by post, managed to convince our parents that we were not staying and left under somewhat of a cloud with neither of our parents wishing to make anything of our hasty retreat. So ended my career as a budding farmer. I never heard of or saw my friend again.

Chapter 2

Once more into the breach

It was wonderful to get home and be civilized. However, unbeknown to me, Dad and my Uncle had received a second reply this time from a farmer in Wiltshire. As the Shropshire one seemed much nearer and apparently the correspondence had seemed in order, it had been decided that indeed that one had been the better option. But after a somewhat fraught few days I found myself one morning en route to Frome in Wiltshire, with all my baggage accompanying me as well.

What a difference this was to be. Mr and Mrs Dyke and their two sons were a great family and later that afternoon and after a lovely meal Mum and Dad left, well content, that this was the place for me. Several weeks passed and I was into everything. I loved it and no one could have welcomed me more heartily However, like it or not I was unable to carry on as I had chronic asthma.

The Dyke family were kindness itself, but after seeking medical attention and discussions with home there seemed no alternative but to abort my farming career. After almost three months which I had enjoyed to the best of my ability and in spite of my asthma, I said goodbye to my new found friends. I was sent home by an ambulance car. It obviously was not going to be the life for me and I was bitterly disappointed. What was I going to do next if I was to escape going into the family business as a tailor and outfitter? The thought that this might happen filled me with horror.

By chance a friend of the family, who was in the Merchant Navy, was on leave. At the time he was second mate on some ship in the Indian Ocean and seen by my parents as a bit of a rogue. I must say he did seem to have a tale beyond belief to tell. Not the sort of life that you would call an assurance to my parents. Nevertheless it might well be a start for me. I might say as a young fellow, I was completely fascinated with all that he recounted.

TELEPHONE Nº 2137.

S.R.PULLINGER, M.A.,
HEAD MASTER.

THE GRAMMAR SCHOOL,
LOUGHBOROUGH.

19th October, 1946.

T. J. Bailey was a pupil at this School from September 1939 to December 1945. He was very severely handicapped in his early years by ill-health, which caused him to lose a great deal of time in his School work so that his progress through the School was slow and he did not get as far as most boys of his age when, on grounds of ill-health, he left to take up an open air life in farming.

He was an active, well-developed lad and took a very keen part in all activities out of doors: being also a live member of one of the town scout groups. Although he has not got very far in mathematics he has a fair foundation on which to build, and, with better health and the ability to concentrate on his work, he should be able to cope with such study as is needed for the Merchant Navy. He is the type of boy well-suited to a nautical career and I am very glad to recommend him on grounds of character for the apprenticeship which he is seeking.

S. R. Pullinger

Headmaster Sid Pullinger's fateful letter

5

It was then that the idea came to me that a job at sea might fill the bill. This is where Dad thought there was a way to at least getting me started with some prospects for the future. Letters were written to all the well known shipping companies possibly with a view to an apprenticeship. The standard reply always came back the same "What school had I been to?" That was easy. But when it came to qualifications, well, I did not have any. One evening Dad called me into the lounge. Apparently, a letter from my old headmaster had arrived hoping that I might find some outlet in my life which was really devoid of any academic qualification. "Look here, Jim," Dad said, having read and re-read Mr Pullinger's fateful message, "Mr Trowbridge your old form master has contacted me with a view to coming to see if he could help in any way with your studies."

So, Mr Trowbridge had actually offered to help me. It was incredible. Trowy, who was a Quaker, lived down the road with his wife and was now retired. I was amazed that he was willing to help someone like myself whose schooling had almost been a disaster. This was a wonderful stroke of luck.

Before long a campaign had been launched and put on the table with Trowy in attendance. The rules were quite simple. Providing I was prepared to give it my all and keep my head down to some really hard studying he would give me free tuition for four hours a week. "How does that sound, Jim?" I thanked him profusely and after he had left Dad gave me a very serious talking to. I had to agree that it was indeed a last ditch stand if I was to make any way in life.

Later that evening which seemed an eternity, Dad called me into the lounge. "Sit down, Jim," and trembling unbelievably I obeyed. "Jim," said Dad, "Mr Trowbridge has had a long talk with your mother and I and it is his opinion that if you are prepared to buckle down and study and it is what you would like to do then he is prepared to do his part."

All hands to the pump

The rest of the evening was spent in planning my studies, mostly maths, which was to consist of four evenings a week, each one of two hours, quite naturally at his home. This had to be taken into consideration as both Mr and Mrs Trowbridge were very private people. That night after Trowy had gone we all three sat down and, as might be expected, considered the rather unusual day's events. We thanked God for this unusual turn of events, it was a real chance for me to at least get started. But what had not been said was that Trowy, on saying goodnight to Dad, said that he would not accept payment. That was an incredible stroke of good fortune.

The next few months flew by. Trowy was giving me more and more work to do. Life was at last beginning to flow and I loved it. Then one day a letter came through the letter box addressed to Mr Norman Bailey accepting his son T. J. Bailey to sit the entrance exam the following week, at the nautical college at Warsash. The exam would be in two parts. It was requested that I was to arrive in good time as a number of candidates would be sitting the exam on that day.

I can only imagine the scene that ensued on Dad's return that lunch time. My mother, who was a very quiet lady, apparently showed a completely new side to her nature. Dad had apparently decided without consulting anyone that as the reports from Trowy had been most favourable, that without any further discussion he felt that it was high time I was tested. Therefore, without further adieu he had applied to the Nautical College at Warsash, near Southampton.

Off to Warsash Nautical Establishment

Whether I agreed or not, I found myself one week later on board a train via London to Southampton, to stay the night at a local pub, ready for my big challenge the next day.

I was terrified, but in those days young people did as their parents wanted them to do. However, as I felt I had been such a disaster to date, could it be I was actually getting somewhere at last? The interesting part of all this was that Dad had informed Trowy of his intention. What Trowy said, I was not party to, I can only imagine that he was most surprised.

I must say I was more than flattered by any possibility of me even remotely being able to pass any kind of exam, but on the other hand there was a certain feeling of pride that Dad thought I had the remotest chance of success. In my mind this had to be a plus.

The following morning I presented myself at Warsash and along with four other candidates sat the exam.

The invigilator was a petty officer who was obviously retired and thank goodness not too high-powered. At the end of the three hours our papers were removed, food vouchers were issued and we were asked to present ourselves in the waiting room afterwards.

I must say I was desperately trying to remember the morning's paper. Certainly the paper about the rule of the road with practical answers applicable, I found easy. But the theory paper I knew would be a disaster. So the wait, for how long I knew not, seemed interminable. Eventually the door opened and the petty officer came and informed the other four candidates that they may go. Looking at me he indicated I should follow him.

It didn't take much for me to realise that this was it. I knocked on the door marked "Commander" and walked in. Almost before the door had closed the occupier of the chair was talking. In his hand, he had the application form that Dad had forwarded. The Commander eyed me up and down and waving the paper he commenced, "May I ask you, Sir, what right have you coming here so ill equipped. Your father's writing I assume?" He then just dismissed me, with the aside, "I will be writing to him." And so ended my nautical start.

I was pleased that night to get home, but not so pleased to have to report the obvious. However, that evening it was agreed by Dad, Mum and me, that it had been an experience and to an extent a learning curve. But surely one I could have done without. Now my confidence was at an all time low.

A few days later a letter arrived making it quite plain to Dad the situation, which Mum heartily endorsed. If she had been consulted initially she would have said that I needed more time to improve my nautical knowledge before being tested. After a few days' recuperation and now determined to have learned a lesson from this past experience, I picked up my studies again. I have to say without the aid of Trowy, who quite rightly had thrown in the towel. After all he was now in his late sixties and ready to completely retire. Dad and I went along to his house to thank him for all his support. As he did not drink, we presented his wife with a bunch of flowers. So here ends another saga in the life of would-be Sailor Jim.

Deviation

In 1939 I joined the Nanpantan scouts and during the war we all helped where we could with what were called the civil

A proud King's Scout

defence and St John Ambulance. Saturday mornings would see the Badger patrol, of which I was a member, going down to the drill hall where we all became guinea pigs for the St John Ambulance. This involved picking up a card issued to us. Probably we were to be walking wounded, or we had a broken back or were badly burnt, whichever it was. We were in one of the derelict buildings where first aiders and Red Cross duly came along and attended to our wounds

9

getting practice in for future emergencies. During this time a lot of friends were made.

Amongst these was a scout master who had been in the London blitz. It was through him, that I acquired accommodation at Roland House the scout hostel in Stepney Green in the East End, which now enabled me to enter Sir John Cass, the nautical college in Jury Street just off Tower Hill. Everyone assumed that I was now capable of passing an interview into the college.

To enter the course I had to again go for this interview. I had now really settled in to a work ethic, which without this skill I was never going to get anywhere. I passed the interview alright, but it was based on the fact that I must find a shipping company to take me on. I was given three months to sort this out. All the other students had already been accepted but I had a smug feeling, that maybe, the college thought I was worth a try.

| THE SIR JOHN CASS TECHNICAL INSTITUTE |
| JEWRY STREET, ALDGATE, E.C.3. |
| MEMBER'S TICKET |
| *(Not Transferable)* |
| SESSION 1946-47. |
| No. M.1602 |
| *Name* Mrs. T. J. Bailey. |
| *Address* |
| *Date of Issue* 15 APR 1947   FEE PAID 1/- |

A college 'boy' at last.

The big plus for me as an only child, was that I was now mixing with some fine company lads. The majority of them had school certificates, a far cry from me. However, my survival was dependent on my obtaining a position in a shipping company immediately. This then was the number one priority.

Roland House

Of course the other great bonus was the fact that I was now living at Roland House. I believe it was probably built for a sea captain in the 16th century and in those days it would have been surrounded by fields. It had indeed been a magnificent home with large rooms, all of which were panelled in wood and must have had magnificent views of the Thames. The story goes that a certain captain's wife spent her time sitting at the window of the dormitory we were in, waiting for her husband to return from his long sea voyages.

Our lives at Roland House were governed by a Mrs Caldwell. She was a lady in her 50s called 'Ma' by everyone. We were her surrogate family. Do her right and all was well with the world, do her wrong and you wished you had never left home. A formidable but fair lady!

Roland House – what a grand start.

Bearing in mind that it was 1946 and everything was in short supply and most shops were empty, Ma's table was the highlight of the day. For returning from the college a good hour's walk away to be met with a mug of tea and wonderful cheese sandwiches was very special.

We all had duties to do in the hostel, which were allotted by Ma. We paid the Hostel the magnificent sum of one pound ten shillings a week. I required one pound twelve shillings for my return rail fare to Loughborough this left me one pound for everything else. As I smoked a pipe even then, some of this was spent on tobacco and of course the odd drink. Apart from the London transport, buses and lorries there was really hardly any movement of traffic. Amazingly the underground was working well. Everywhere everything was requiring attention, but considering the enormous battering that London had received, you could only admire the tenacity and spirit of the Londoners. I must say due to my lack of finances, Shank's Pony had to do for me.

Nothing like cheese 'sarnies'

The dormitory which I had been allocated to had a very mixed bag of lads. We were, of all ages, I was the youngest and Burt (the only name I can still remember) was in his fifties. We had a bank clerk, a street trader or two, students at various colleges and a ballet dancer from the Royal Ballet. Imagine Ma trying to deal with us, but what fun we had.

What a fine room to learn 'the rules of the road'.

Chapter 3

This could be it!

About three months into the course, a letter arrived from Lamport & Holt Line, whose offices were in the Royal Liver Buildings in Liverpool. They were a cargo passenger line.

It was in answer to one of the many shipping companies that Dad and I had written too, in the hope of a response. This letter was inviting me to go for an interview. I don't think any of us could take it all in. Hopefully I was on my way.

One morning in July 1947 Dad and I drove over the top of Derbyshire en route for Liverpool and the Royal Liver Buildings for my interview with Lamport & Holt Line. Grandpa Bailey's old Austin 12 car had been spruced up for the occasion and with Dad at the wheel and myself sorted out by Mum in, a pair of Dad's grey trousers let out at the waist (as I was a bigger build than him) and a clydella shirt with the collar turned, I started to look the part of a young 16 year old on his way to a future life.

Anyone reading this might well imagine the clothes were all handed down. It was a make-do-and-mend job all down the line. Surprisingly nobody seemed to bother about it. How different to our grandchildren of today!

Anyway back to the immediate situation...

The journey over Derbyshire was most interesting as little had been done since the war to try to get back to normality. The road sides were littered with corrugated huts where ammunition had been dispersed. It was almost two years since the end of the war and the huts were still full of ammunition, minus their charges of course.

The approach to Liverpool was something else. Half the city seemed to have been bombed with whole streets devastated. We made our way down towards the river, where the Royal Liver Buildings were, just in front of the landing stage, which was to become so familiar to me in the years to come.

Straight ahead of us we observed the Liver Buildings, tall and majestic with the Hugh Liver Bird standing proudly on the top, probably twenty or thirty feet in height and painted in gold. We had arrived!

The Royal Liver Building

Many ships lay at anchor with their company flags flying. Others had courtesy flags if they were from abroad. Some were preparing to go to sea with pilots on board and others were waiting for high tide to move into the docks.

Tugs plied hither and thither and ferries wended their way between, on their way from Spilers wharf on the Cheshire side over to the landing stage in front of the Liver Buildings. Such was the excitement of it all. At one time, presumably in the middle of the last century, there would have been sailing brigs as well as steamers plying their way. It was all very exciting and nostalgic. Dad and I walked along to the pier observing all that was going on. However by the '20s most of the sail had vanished and everything went to power-driven vessels.

Just off the main front, we saw the entrance to Lamport & Holt Line, like all these buildings they were very grand. We mounted the steps and for just a second Dad put his hand on my shoulder and said, "Good luck. Go for it Jim."

William James Lamport 1815-1874

George Holt 1824-1896.

The building itself completely over-awed both of us, probably built in the early 1820s when William James Lamport and George Holt came together to form the company. Just think that the Battle of Waterloo was only five years before on June 18th, 1815.

A whole book could be written about these wonderful founders of the merchant fleet. The first ships were three or four hundred tonnes, built of wood and with little lifesaving gear or appliances to help them. Time would be dictated by the wind. No wind no sailing, so ship owners would have to rely heavily on the weather for ships arriving or leaving port. However by the mid-19th century, steam was coming in and this had the advantage of making arrivals in ports more reliable and of course ships were being built of iron. The combination of a ship under steam and sail must have been a fine sight.

The most remarkable thing of all is that from these two gentlemen other shipping companies were formed. Some of them like the Blue Funnel Line being of the finest standards and where loyalty and pride were very much in evidence.

I go for an interview

So we turned into the main doors of the Royal Liver Building to find ourselves at the bottom of a magnificent staircase, as we proceeded upwards to the main office.

Dad nudged me, "Look," he said pointing to the walls, "What do you think about that?" It was an amazing sight with all the walls covered in black boards. I suppose this is considered politically incorrect by today's standards. However that was what they were. Each one was headed by the name of one of the companies and underneath the name and the whereabouts of the ship, its time of sailing from the next port, and any other relevancies for that ship.

The names were magic, Rio de Janeiro, Bahia, New York. The places I had dreamed about visiting were all there.

"Mr Bailey, Sir." A very pleasant gentleman addressed me, "would you please come this way. The chairman will see you now. By the way, the chairman is Mr Lowe." The next moment I found myself in the board room, (for that was what it said on the door) shaking hands with this tiny little man wearing a grey suit wing collar and cravat. "Let's see," he said, perusing the paper he had in his hand, "Ah, yes you are at present in London at Sir John Cass." Looking up he said, "Are you enjoying it?" I assured him that I was. "And you think a life at sea is the one for you?" What could I reply to that?

"Well," he continued, "The report from the college sees you as keen and hard working." How grateful I was for those few encouraging words. Carrying on, he said, "As you are no doubt aware, you may have to wait some time for a ship – on the other hand they may need you tomorrow, so prepare yourself for this and check you have all the necessary injections. Providing you don't cause any hassle or upsets I shall not expect to see you for four years when your time as a cadet will be finished. Good luck, lad." And with that I thanked him and left.

Dad and I walked quietly down the stairs to where the wonderful model of the *Vandyke*, a magnificent passenger liner, was encased. Little did I realise that its sister ship was lost many moons before. Neither of us unable to contain ourselves it all came out, "Well, my lad." It was not necessary to say any more. He put his hand on my shoulder and just said, "Keep your nose clean, Jim, and you have a job for life. Well done, but from now on you are on your own, the world is your oyster. Good!"

I leave Roland House

I returned to Roland House to finish the course at the college well aware that I could be called at any time to join a ship, which of course could be anywhere in the world. Mum had taken the precaution of checking all my clothes, which seemed somewhat excessive but then I had working gear, uniform, which basically consisted of battle dress which was the standard for cadets plus work gear, plus tropical kit.

The last day at the college came and still no boat. Bearing in mind that for the last eighteen months I had dreamed of such a moment when I might enter a shipping office the reader might possibly comprehend some of the nerves I was currently suffering. I was so totally overawed by the size of everything that was happening around me that for a few moments I completely lost my reasoning for being there.

Others were also leaving Roland House and so home for Christmas we decided to take Ma out on a binge before saying goodbye. Not being used to this sort of thing, we had to engineer the evening by a few drinks down Ma at the house first. To put in a nutshell, Ma was singing us all the cockney songs like you never heard before and to be sure the next morning we were all given a right telling off. However, like most big-hearted ladies, when it came time to say goodbye she was almost inconsolable at the thought of us leaving.

So ended my spell in London. I had learnt an awful lot and enjoyed every minute of it. When I think back on those times I thank Ma for giving us an aspect on life, which I believe came from mixing with so many different sorts of people and learning all about their business in the daytime, then home to Roland house and Ma. Before you had got in the door, there would be a yell from the kitchen asking who it was and if you were unlucky enough to be on the duty rota for that night you were promptly reminded of it.

Actually I don't think anyone would have had it any other way, because rationing was still on and the sooner we got to the meal on table, which Ma, conjured up from goodness knows where, it was a dream come true. It was gannets to the fore. All meals were sent up from the kitchen by a service lift and the room we ate in was part of the old house, all panelled in oak. One could imagine what it must have been like in the 17/18th century.

Much of the house was really derelict and you had to walk up those wide wooden stairs to our dormitory, with everything creaking was something else. There was a great lack of lighting. In fact most of the corridors were in total darkness. I suppose there were about twenty rooms, all of which were panelled. I wish now that I had had a camera, but there you are we didn't think of things like that then.

Down below in the cellar, somewhere along the line in the past, someone had had a small chapel built, seating about a dozen people. Actually, it had a rather old but workable organ, that with the aid of someone working the bellows a chap called Simon then could play it. I remember him clearly for his

19

drinking habits. We all drank to some extent of course. Unfortunately we had no money so between us we concocted some vile stuff. This was with the aid of Ma's husband who was adept at making home-made booze. I was violently sick and I wasn't the only one either. Certainly with only twenty-five shillings a week to spend you had to be content with anything.

The chapel – note the size

I think the one outstanding memory of those days, was that London had frequent pea-soupers, dense fog. This was due to many factors, smoke and little attention in those days was paid to the environment. Anyhow it was on one of these pea-souper mornings, that I sallied forth with my rucksack on my back to set off to the Nautical College which would take me up the Mile End Road, past the London Hospital to Aldgate. I had a job to see the pavement under my feet. Quite frankly, I would have been better employed staying at the hostel and doing some studying there. Nothing seemed to be moving anyway.

Trying to get my bearings, as a sailor should, with eyes down I came to an abrupt halt having walked into something. Anyone who has experienced this will know how I felt. Completely dazed and almost knocked out.

After a few minutes of trying to collect myself and with a very sore head, I found myself clutching an upright bar. This turned out to be the handle you grab when getting onto a double-decker bus. It appeared to be lying at right angles across the pavement. With the passengers having disembarked as the driver had given up in these conditions, he must have fallen asleep, but my yell of pain had woken him up. To cut a long story short, I agreed to walk in front of the bus, with one foot in the gutter and one on the pavement; so we set off, with the bus not more than a yard behind me. It took all morning to travel the mile or so to our destination at Aldgate. I vowed that "Once was enough" and the driver totally agreed.

Chapter 4

I join Lamport & Holt Line

I well remember on my return to Loughborough for Xmas 1947 at home that it was the first time I had got anywhere and now all I wanted was a ship. I went for walks with Mum, who gave me the never ending guff about remembering to "change your socks regularly and don't let your hair get too long," all of which I took note. She was a funny old thing really, but I do believe then that we had a good understanding.

Almost the next day the long awaited letter came through the letter box, informing me to go down to Lamport & Holt's London office in the New Year when I would be directed as to the whereabouts of the ship I was to join, the S.S. *Lalande*. Then of course we had no phone. If we had had one I would have rung the company for a few more details. In fact we never had one in the house until the spring of 1948. So the old Christmas ritual was gone through and we went down to mother's parents for the festivities. My grandfather presented me with a wonderful old Measham pipe, in a case lined in silk, with instructions that when I found an old bosun, with the accent on the word 'old', I was to say it was from him, along with a fiver that Gran gave me. Lucky bosun was what I thought. Now I was all ready for foreign parts.

So on a filthy foggy morning in early January, I found myself on Loughborough L.M.S. station with my trunk and all the requirements for an old sea dog and my brand new peak cap with the L.H. badge on it, I felt the bee's knees.

Coming from a country town, as it was in those days, I was never very happy in London, even after the six months in

Stepney. Still I suppose it was hardly fair to compare one with the other. I was well aware that it was wrong to compare the East End with home. However, basically I was an open-air lad with a love of fields and woods to roam around in. I had always had to remind myself that there were those who had never seen those things and more than once I had found myself in conflict with the friends I had made whilst living at Roland House. I reflected on these things as the train rolled down to London and the conclusion I came to was how lucky I had been to have had this adventure and people like Ma would never be forgotten

My destination was just off Leadenhall Street and so I duly arrived there.

The London Office

This was nothing like their Liverpool one and on presenting myself to the desk, which was very informal I gave my name and the letter reference my joining the *Lalande*.

This was, apparently news to them. Anyway after a phone call, I assumed this was to the Liverpool office, my existence was established. I was then told my ship was lying down the Thames at Grays.

The office was without much lighting, very typical of many establishments that had not brought themselves out of the dim war years. I noticed once again how dismal the city was, ever so dark and morbid. The lighting in the office was terrible.

Consequently, I was unaware of a figure sitting on a couch in the corner of the office. I took my seat to await transport down to the ship; the S.S. *Lalande* was apparently lying in the river.

The Master, or 'old man' as the Captain of a merchant ship is known, was to be my companion down to the river, not that I realised this at the time, as no introduction was offered by the office staff and there was no indication as to whom he might be.

Mr. T.J. Bailey,
101 Beacon Road,
Loughborough,
Leics.

Dear Sir,

        Thank you for your letter of the
14th instant.

        I am sorry to find that I shall
have to go to the Continent next week and
shall not be available in London until
Thursday or Friday 23rd or 24th, but I
have arranged for you to be interviewed
by Mr. Hayes and shall be glad if you will
kindly ask for this gentleman when you call
on Wednesday next.

                    Yours faithfully,

                        London Manager.

Had I been aware that this tiny, rather scruffy figure was indeed my future Captain to be, it is doubtful, indeed highly improbable that I would have dared to have done anything but stand in his company. I was to realise many years later, what an important role he was to play in my life. Full of anecdotes and tales of wisdom, he was a pleasure to be with, a realist, a good sense of humour, but very firm.

He was a square rig master. He served his time in square rigged ships. His father sailed under sail too and rose to be Skipper, as they were then called. How this quiet little man could make such an impression on we lads in the future and how much he became indelibly marked on my memory, is something I would never forget. He was a most remarkable person indeed. Anyway back to the present. As there was no indication as to who he was sitting there in a raincoat and cloth cap, I said "Good morning." Receiving no reply, I plonked myself down to await the transport.

Off to see my ship at last

To be honest with you I cannot remember much about the trip down to Grays. There was nothing to see, as it was dense fog again, so that you had a job to see the bonnet of the taxi. The cabbie, with his head out of the window, was trying to gauge where we were.

After what seemed to be an age, we stopped, the cabbie doing his best to pacify the old man that to go on would be madness. I was to find out that the old man, like his contemporaries, found it very difficult to accept no for an answer however foolish. Suffice it is to say we were lucky that with the daylight fading rapidly we had actually arrived at an old quay where a rowing boat was awaiting the old man and of course yours truly.

Through the fast approaching gloom and fog I could just see the outline of a merchant ship, with its massive funnel and two masts bristling with derricks. With time running out, we were both soon on board the boat to take us out and with my trunk in the stern we did not look the most seamen-like expedition. Within ten minutes we were alongside the gangway. The old man was away like a shot for all his age and with the aid of one of the crew I found myself aboard the merchant ship S.S *Lalande*. Had I had arrived at last on this wonderful steamship?

This is not exactly the way to introduce oneself to the wonderful life of the sea which I had so long waited for, especially as I had my brand new uniform on that had been so carefully tended by mother that morning. She would say, "We must not let the side down." By now it was getting dark and without any knowledge of the layout on board, I was some what confused. The shore boat that had brought us over had gone. The old man who went aboard first had vanished and there was but one small light up the alleyway which meant absolutely nothing to me. In fact the ship seemed dead. I was to learn later that day that the ship had been at the buoys waiting for cargo for the last week. Consequently apart from a skeleton crew, the rest were on leave and were not expected to arrive back until the following morning.

The steamer "Lalande", built by D. and W. Henderson and Co. Ltd., in 1920.

J. McRoberts collection

The format on a merchant ship is fairly consistent and obviously small ships have fewer crew on board. We were a medium sized vessel. The *Lalande*, which was a good average size for a merchant ship, was built in 1920s. She was a ship of 7500 tonnes having a crew of twenty-five consisting of: master, three deck officers, some cadets and around twelve deck hands, including bosun and carpenter.

The Engineering dept consists of a chief engineer, 2nd eng and 3rd eng. This is to cover a twenty-four hour day, as indeed the same is for the deck officers. We had the Chief Steward who rules over the galley and all stewards. As you can imagine that on large passenger ships, this is the largest department on board. In our case as a general cargo vessel we had a total crew of twenty-five, as we had to do much of our own deck work, especially on the North Brazilian ports.

I well remember the call from the first mate. We three cadets were just finishing our lunch, which I might say looked a little unappetising. Still I must say it was to be something of a regular grumble with we three cadets.

s/s Lalande
24.2.48

Menu

Breakfast

Chilled Paw Paw

Rolled Oats   All Bran

Grilled Manx Kipper

Poached Egg on Toast

Curried Beef & Rice

Preserves   Tea   Coffee   Cocoa

Curry for breakfast!

When you are hungry you are very glad to have what is going, and when the first mate asks for your presence, you are usually quick to obey. It is amazing, how you remember all these things so many years later!

Before carrying on any further with what I loosely call my story, I think I should explain to the possible reader, (if there are any?) that I am no computer buff. Indeed if you were to be unlucky to observe my work on the computer to date you would find a mixture of large and small print, which does nothing to help my skills in attempting to write all this. Indeed, it is my first attempt.

Had one of our grandchildren been about, things might have been easier for me and clearer for you. Anyway three years as a cadet on board a merchant ship without doubt, in changing times, as the war finished and in my case a chance to go to Brazil was something I could only have dreamt about a few weeks before. As we were finishing our meal we were informed that the mate, Mr Spooner, wished to see us. We downed tools and made our way to his cabin just below the Captain's cabin under the bridge.

I found Captain Purton, Polly to us all, was a very fair man over the time I sailed with him, but you could not mess with him either. In other words you were left in no doubt as to the relationship he required from we lads and it worked well. He was a very different character to another master who I was to sail under at the end of the following year.

Mr Spooner, the Chief Officer, alias first mate invited us in to the dining room, which was now cleared. After the initial "Hullo" and "What have you done?" this meant which college and ships had we been on and other relevant information. Then speaking to Brian who had sailed with him before, he introduced us to him and gave his position as senior cadet. All three of us were then given a briefing with regard to our status on board, which in my case didn't much inform me of the immediate situation or what would be expected of me.

We were to complete loading cement for the next two or three days then we were to proceed to Glasgow for general cargo and lastly to our home port of Liverpool to complete the voyage.

He then went on to say that we would not necessarily be working watches. This would depend on how far ahead the ship was prepared for Glasgow our next port. Also the problems with the boiler were far from sorted. He then explained to us that the *Lalande* was now twenty-seven years old and had survived the war well, However, as he observed, we still had a gun on the after deck armaments. Around the whole ship was heavy-duty wire cable called 'degaussing gear' which runs right round the deck. This was used to help detract mines in the water by a reverse current being put through the electric cable. At that time it was not possible to remove any of this due to the time factor on arriving in Liverpool. Mr Spooner, we never used first names on board, then went on to say he wouldn't tolerate any slacking and then gave us our duties.

I later realised he was a very human being but nevertheless very firm and I believe the three of us found no problem with that. However it was the senior cadet, Brian who was the contact we liaised with from now on. There was much to be done. I have to say after our very civilized talk with Mr Spooner, I was somewhat shocked to find that Brian suddenly hardened to the two of us and a list of work as long as your arm was foisted on to us. I resolved there and then, that I would try to be a much fairer Senior Cadet if I ever reached such dizzy heights. Little did I realise then, that this would happen in the not so distant future.

It was then explained to us by Brian that he was the one who carried the can and this was so. I remember, when I was senior cadet, the awful thought of having to be hauled up before the mate for something that I had not done. In this case it was the duty of the senior cadet to deal with the situation. I remember it well, as I was stopped a month's wages for the lack of foresight by a new cadet. How about that! I have to say in defence it rarely happened.

The order of the day was scrubbing decks, and polishing brass work, which was done with sand and water. A very tight budget was kept and slacking was not tolerated. All a bit tough when you first joined but never mind, it kept your mind off other things such as missing home. We soon found out that the daily ritual was a hose down from the bridge deck to the after end of the boat deck. This deck had the skylights for the engine room some thirty feet below where the lifeboats were, consisting of two on either side. The reason for this is that if you had had to abandon ship, there are always sufficient lifeboats on one side for all the crew to get off comfortably.

We had ten derricks on board, all capable of handling most cargo. In the event of there being really heavy loads, such as a railway engine, then this would all be handled by shore cranes This could obviously cause trouble, if for instance, we were unable to go alongside in a designated port. In such a case we would either have to go to the nearest port where facilities were capable of handling this or as happened, not very frequently, the ship took the risk, something that would not be allowed today. Then the ship had to be re-rigged to cope with the extra weight. I think I should explain that although safety was always uppermost on board, that this was a very old ship coming through the war apparently unscathed. But maintenance was in those days minimal, purely because the main consideration was to get a vessel out loaded, onto its next port of call.

During the War many vessels barely left port before being torpedoed. Sadly what also should be remembered is that in many cases that crews were not picked up because any other ship offering its services would be a sitting duck. So they simply did not take this risk.

Lamport & Holt lost 60% of its ships during this time. Could anyone ever imagine the grief felt by loved ones and indeed the company staff at the Royal Liver Buildings who had the task of informing loved ones and next of kin.

Many of the seamen came from the pool. This was where all crews were picked according to their disciplines. Many shipping companies used this method of obtaining crew. Others became company men with some of them becoming permanent crew. Anyway, three days after I joined the ship, with a full complement on board and everything stowed, I found myself on the fo'c'sle with a hose in my hand washing down, as the anchor was winched in by the carpenter, as I said earlier 'Chippy' to us all. The ship's siren blew the all clear as we turned in the river helped by tugs and slowly I felt the ship throb as we got underway.

It was a wonderful moment as we passed slowly down the river with the red and white H Flag denoting a pilot on board. The first mate blew down the pipe to the bridge. for that was all the means we had for communicating, to say that we were all clear forward, I felt the throb of the boat as the engines increased speed. It was magic! However it was only momentarily, for there was work to be done, the hatches to be battened down and derricks to be covered, lowered and fastened, decks cleared and washed down. All this was required at all times. There was always the fear of fire on board, particularly when carrying cargoes of cotton which was a regular problem as when stowed tightly it could self ignite. There were many different ways of carrying and securing cargo. For instance in the case of cotton, all steel work below decks had to be covered in wood to stop the cotton sweating and getting soiled by the steel sides of the ship. The sad part was that most of this timber was mahogany and in most cases was dumped at sea after leaving our final port outward bound. Rich pickings perhaps for South American beachcombers.

I was given the middle watch, that is from midday to 4pm and midnight to 4am, which was all a bit of a worry to me. It was because of the second officer, the navigation officer, who I do not wish to name. I am sure he was a very good officer. However, from the start he and I never saw eye to eye and to be on watch with him was not quite what a first-time cadet really wanted. Never mind, as I have been told a million times, it is all part of the job.

Gradually we proceeded downriver on the last of the flood tide. I could see the lights of London receding, although the glow and later the loom of these lights would be with us for some time. It was a very pleasant evening and I had a long chat with Brian about the do's and don'ts on board about which he was most vehement. His advice was never to go on watch without the right clothing. The reason he gave for this was that as I was on the midnight to 4am with my friend the second mate, who always preferred to see us outside when on watch. His excuse being that you could not see through the glass of the bridge if you were merely a lookout. What a nice gentleman!

Personally, I called it just common sense, but then who was I, a mere junior cadet to argue, Not being able to sleep and with a mixture of excitement and now looking to the future, I thought about home and wondered what they were all doing. Thinking back those many years ago, it was all rather emotional. My mind also turned to Roland House and Ma. What a great lady and friend she had been. All those cheese sandwiches and the telling off when we all became too boisterous. To all of us who stayed at the scout hostel there was no one like Ma. She was definitely a surrogate mother of the finest kind.

The light was dwindling fast as we snaked round and down the Thames on the last of the flood tide, outward bound. I could see other lights now and buoys flashing, denoting the channel we were to take. The river seemed so wide now as the water filled the banks. On either side small and big ships were plying their way. Tugs were hooting, denoting their intentions and large vessels passed bound in and out of the channel. I had as yet not been called to the bridge for any duties, so for the moment I hung over the rail on the portside watching the world go by.

Chapter 5

Learning fast

The only time I had ever been to this part of the world had been before the war when a day trip had been organised down to Southend by our local Congregational church. I remember walking along the pier with a real old boy, who having obtained our attention then proceeded to tell us this fascinating story. How in the early days when all ships were made of timber, that the forests up the River Stour where all the tallest oaks stood, some of them many hundreds of years old, provided this timber. And of how they were felled and hulls were built on the side of the river and then launched. Then they were rowed down the river and across the Thames, not far from where we were, and round the Isle of Grain and up to the Royal Navy Docks at Chatham, where they were rigged out as "men of war". How fascinating to think that we were actually at the cross roads of those times.

For myself it was the start of a great adventure passing slowly downriver with all the deck lights off and just the navigation lights on, I knew this was indeed what I had been looking for. Without another thought in my head I made a bee line for our cabin and a good night's sleep. It had been a great day. Our cabin was on the starboard side at the rear end of the accommodation, amidships, measuring three metres square, not very big when you think that we three could be living in it for up to two years at a time. For in those days we were on two year articles and could be kept out for as long as that. There were three bunks, obviously, one either side, with the one allocated to me above. I was so close to the deck head, the ceiling, that is was necessary for me to bend almost double.

To put it in a nutshell it was not possible to sit upright. My sympathy was with all those guys that had been the occupant of this particular bunk since 1920. We had one small wardrobe between us and two drawers each.

Now this is crunch time. We had to go down the alley way some twenty feet to wash and go to the toilets, sharing with eight others. Of course what I didn't know was that directly over my bunk was a steam winch, but it wouldn't take long for me to realise this. Had I been more experienced I would have seen this at the start, still we live and learn.

My first full day at sea will be something I shall always remember, called as I was at 7am, now being assigned to day duty. It was amazing to watch the ship plying along at a comfortable ten knots and only half loaded.

It was a lovely morning and, as far as I can remember, remained fine throughout the next few days. By the morning we were out of the Thames estuary and had altered course to go north and round the top of Scotland, through the Pentland Firth and thence down to Glasgow. As I was not a party to any of this I could only enjoy the various points we passed, in between working of course. There would be plenty of time too, in the future for navigation. To be perfectly honest I really remember nothing about Glasgow, the old man was determined to load and get out as quickly as possible. We were working flat out, quite a lot of it heavy work. Consequently as soon as I had finished it was into my bunk post-haste.

So before I realised it we were on our way to Liverpool and word had got out that there might be some leave on our arrival there.

During the trip round to Liverpool I was introduced to most of the deck duties As the junior I received all the filthy jobs, in fact for one whole day I was shoved in the 'tween decks. That is a deck between two others shovelling cement – sort of character building, or so I was informed by the bosun. Still not to be outdone I sailored on. When you are living cheek by jowl it pays to keep one's council.

I well remember, it was a Friday morning and there might be a possible chance of me nipping home for a night, as the *Lalande* was due for some boiler maintenance. This did not surprise me as her old double-ended steam Scottish boilers were blowing like fun and in addition the chief engineer, as we were informed later, had told the old man to "stuff his ship" if he didn't get the job sorted out. As yet we were still some way from the entrance to the river Mersey. Formby Sands was a beam to port and now in quieter water all hands were busy rigging derricks, breaking the anchor out should we require it and a general air of expectancy, particularly as this was their home town.

I was just about to walk across to the other side of the boat deck to have a look at Birkenhead, when the third mate yelled at me. "Come here!" he shouted, as I approached the most sacred of places, the bridge itself. I never forgot it as he said "Get a cloth and clean those windows, Bailey." And to think I thought the pilot wanted some advice. Nevertheless, I had made the bridge at last. Actually my duties on arrival and leaving port were to make myself available, but as far as possible not to be invasive, which I took to mean to be seen but not heard. Where had I heard that before, I wondered?

The situation with regard to the ship's master and the pilot is quite simple and that is the pilot is merely there for local knowledge. But in practice the pilot normally takes the vessel in and out of port and in cases an AB who knew the river and docks well would act as quarter master in and out of most ports, with the exception of the Suez Canal and other specific channels, which were totally under a particular port authority. Nevertheless the master was still in charge, a little difficult as you could imagine at times.

We had an old boy from Stonaway who was an incredible "Jock" as he was known. He was the broadest Scott I ever encountered, always drunk in port but once we hit the sea, that was it – a true man of the sea if I ever saw one, a brilliant seaman when splicing wires and rope. He made all his own clothes, shoes as well out of ship's canvas and he was allowed to take the ship through the Gladstone Lock with engines going slow ahead. The only trouble was you couldn't tell a word he said.

However enough of that for now, as we are approaching the Mersey River with Liverpool to port and Birkenhead to starboard, it was almost high tide and we would be going straight into the lock and with tugs fore and aft we turned in the river and into our berth.

I found it hard to believe that only a short time ago Dad and I had motored up through Derbyshire, for my interview with Mr Lowe the chairman of the company. The situation I found myself in couldn't have been more different.

Once alongside, things really began to move; those designated leave were away like a shot, shore gangs were on board taking over the duties of loading and close behind with briefcases came the office crowd from the Liver Buildings discharging some of the old hands. From what I saw they were heavily engrossed with the Chief Steward, who I had observed during my time on board was the key to many activities, a sort of social guru.

As it was now getting on and the weekend was almost upon me, I plucked up courage to have a word with the mate on duty, to see if there was any chance of a weekend off. With a positive reply, I was soon changed and on my way to Lime Street Station and home, Mum and Dad and my own bed was my idea of heaven. There is no substitute for home comforts, with which I was showered aplenty, once my parents got me in the house. That weekend, over sixty years ago, I remember as clear as if it was yesterday. We just pottered about. I never forget it – Mother or Mum as I called her was a funny old stick really, never quite of this world but lovely.

Each time I went away, she used to say, "Just bring me a little something small, dear." In the end she had drawers full of lovely things, bought from various ports I called at during the next ten years. When she died I found that everything I had ever brought home for her had been carefully wrapped up in tissue paper, everything was put away for a rainy day. Such a shame really, still that is how they thought then, possibly the war had some effect on this with rationing and such austerity.

I could not conclude this small Cameo of Mum, with out mentioning the funniest thing that ever happened. I suppose it depends obviously how you see things, but at the time I thought it was hilarious. As we are all aware, in the war food was desperately short so on this particular trip (in actual fact it was the end of this, my first trip abroad), the ship was laid up in Antwerp for repairs and leave was granted. Knowing the food situation at home, I decided to take a full suitcase or at least as much as I was capable of carrying, of tinned fruit which I had seen on a market in Antwerp. It actually was all from America.

I eventually arrived home with all this. Of course one or two tins were given away and the rest, at least a dozen tins, if my memory serves me correctly, were all placed on the top shelf in the pantry for special occasions. Some six years later my parents moved and as I was home on leave I gave them a hand, as you would. It was my unfortunate job to empty the pantry and guess what – all those tins were still there. When I tried to lift them all the bottoms fell out of the tins. So much for "saving for a rainy day" but it is difficult to change any person's way of a life. Still why should you?

The weekend I had at home, gave me the feeling of being an old hand. On board and the return to the *Lalande* was indeed a revelation as to the serious side of the Merchant Navy. Loading had now begun with many different names on the cargo denoting the ports we were going to visit Being of an inquiring nature and curious to see where our impending destinations were to be, I nailed the third mate in one of the alleyways on board one afternoon. After hearing my request he was only too happy to be of assistance and tell me what was happening. At this juncture it was most important information to me as no one else had offered any instruction as to our ports of call or a resume of what we very junior cadets might want to know.

I think it must be difficult for the young people today, and you observe I say young people, to realise the enormous difference placed by society on the young people of my day. Of course changes were coming. It was certainly well into the fifties before the gap was narrowed allowing we young people almost the privileges to speak to our elders without recourse. To being told, it is either "Nothing to do with you, my lad" or a total rebuff. Without doubt the war helped relieve society of many of these old ideas, rightly or wrongly.

Chapter 6

Southbound

With the ship fully loaded at 32ft draught and the pilot on board we sallied forth out of the Gladstone Docks, out into the River Mersey and with slow ahead on the engines headed for the open sea. The other person on the bridge was the compass adjuster. On a ship of this age we only boasted a binnacle, a wet compass on the flying bridge for taking bearings and a dry compass in the wheel house for steering by. Inside these binnacles were many magnets, which were placed at various angles under the compass card and could be withdrawn or added to, to correct the magnetic effect instilled into the ship. By the loading of various cargoes such as the carrying of steel it had a massive effect on the compass. When loading cotton this effect would be reversed. Also as the hull was steel, every alteration of course affected the ability of the correctness of the ship's course. Further errors in the compass occurred because of the earth's natural magnetism called variation. This was affected by the movement of the ship over the ocean floor. All this knowledge was gained at the Nautical College and was one of my favourite subjects as you will no doubt realise. It was a pity all the other lectures did not produce the same enthusiasm in me.

Anyway, with the compasses corrected and now safely out of the river, the pilot and our intrepid compass corrector away, we gave five short blasts and one long one on the ship's whistle and we were away. This was acknowledged by the escorting tug giving the single blast as it returned to port.

I shall never forget the leaving of the River Mersey and seeing Liverpool slowly vanishing astern into the night. I felt sick before we even left the river, so much so that I forgot to change out of my best gear. Hence disaster was to strike. It didn't stop the watch changing at midnight with me on duty. I was informed that if you could breathe, then come rain or shine, seasick or not, I was always to be on duty. I think it turned out to be the worst few days in my life. But change was on the way.

During the next day or so, we cleared the Long Ships lighthouse, the last corner of England. To go out across the mouth of the English Channel and away out to sea, the feeling was fantastic, I always remember the cook leaning over the rail on the port side amidships saying to me, "Well, lad, that's it, now we can have some decent weather," and, "South America here we come." We were scheduled to arrive in Las Palmas in the Canary Islands in about six days' time, but due to unreliable boilers, which was to become the norm, we had altered course for a small Portuguese port, the name which escapes me, to hopefully be able to effect repairs.

This held us up for the best part of a day. The following morning we continued south and it was then that I noticed a number of strange faces on board. I assumed they were on route to Las Palmas but this proved to be a fallacy on my part, for they were still on board prior to arriving in South America. This however was to be made clear later on. The ship seemed to be spending most of its time stopping, starting and going slow ahead. Again we were not really sure what the matter was. However, on a lighter note, the three of us were now eating in the saloon after the officers and engineers had finished. A sort of second sitting, if you wish to be a little more precise.

Tit bits at the table

During the meal times in the saloon, we were able to hear the raised voices of the chief engineer and first mate (Mr Spooner) discussing the life and times of the *Lalande* and some of her war-time escapades. A conclusion was soon drawn up between us three lads that the old girl had been on numerous escapades, including the Russian convoys and apparently, as indeed I mentioned earlier, was never serviced properly. Quite understandable, when during wartime every thing was required afloat if at all possible.

Consequently many ships had been neglected and such was the shortage of shipping at the end of the war that anything that could float was sent out to hopefully procure their old routes. It certainly seemed to convince us three that maybe we would be in for some fun and games before the voyage would end. Nevertheless, after all the trials and tribulations, after about nine days out of Liverpool we would be in the Canary Islands.

However, back to an explanation reference our visitors on board. During the war to escape persecution many people had fled and landed up in Spain, a neutral country during the war. General Franco, dictator of Spain, was himself not the sort to get mixed up with either. Consequently, the people who had escaped tyranny and who were without a country had no option but to escape. To do this meant that they fled without any papers or identity. So they were seen as people with no fixed abode and in effect were not recognised. Homeless as they were and without a country, their only hope was to start afresh somewhere else.

Supernumeries

This was where a ship calling into port could be an answer. The chance of a passage on a ship, providing it was possible to get on board and hide was slim, but some managed it as on the *Lalande*. Providing they could keep out of the way until well out to sea, when it was highly unlikely that the ship would go back, it was a risk worth taking. I suppose they knew that work and food would be given to them whilst on board and a new identity found in South America. The procedure was quite simple. As far as the ship was concerned these people just did not exist. As they were on the ship without papers they were treated as stowaways, otherwise known as supernumeries.

However, they were on board and represented another pair of hands so to this end they were treated as another member of the crew and treated in most cases in a civilised manner. The rub was that all people on board were the responsibility of the master and the consequences of any ship entering port with such people on board would be catastrophic. As these people had no papers, they were not allowed ashore, except to be put into jail and then returned to the ship on leaving. To have the same thing happen at the next port must have been soul destroying. Also there were fines imposed by the authorities on the ship's company.

To hopefully alleviate this problem and it became quite a common practice, ship's masters without making it seem too obvious, would turn a blind eye and in general give as free a passage as possible. They hoped that these poor folks could escape ashore and hopefully integrate into their surroundings without detection. A tall order but it did seem to work as far as I could tell particularly in a massive country like South America.

Chapter 7

Bunkering in Las Palmas

One early morning Las Palmas appeared ahead and we prepared to round the long jetty which acted as a breakwater as well. There, lying a head of us with the company funnel of black white and blue, was another old lady homeward bound and like us she was taking on fuel. The *Lalade*, I presume had been converted to oil. Across the harbour were all the oil tanks with names like BP, SHELL, ESSO, on them, the whole place was a hive of industry. One thing I did notice was the amount of Catholic nuns and priests on the quayside. Apparently this was to be something all those visiting Las Palmas expected to see.

Each ship as it came alongside would be greeted by a priest or two, accompanied by nuns with push carts. The idea being, that ships (more those homeward bound than outward bound) might well be in need of spiritual help after the escapades ashore in foreign ports. I must make it quite plain here, that this was only my experience and I believe that as many ships were outward bound from Liverpool there were always some Irish crew members on board.

So, the priest would come on board to see if his flock wished to receive penance, and after absolution was granted with the priest using a cabin or some quiet spot on board to do this. It was then that food or other articles were allowed to go ashore on the nuns' hand carts.

I must say I found all this rather bizarre. Still that is only my opinion and I had a lot to learn about life. Certainly there were many Catholics on board so one service was given and another repaid.

The incredible thing to me was that at no time was any of this kind of transaction ever explained to me either. The priest seemed to have done what was required. We were alongside for the afternoon and what mail there was and any information from the agent came aboard. We cast off, saying "Bon Voyage." Having discharged the pilot, which was mandatory, we gave the customary farewell on the rather old ship's whistle.

Away at last

So we set course for South America. At last we were away for real foreign parts now with Las Palmas behind us and a distance of 2500 miles to go. The ship could settle down to a good run and with a fair wind and a sound boiler we should be in Rio in ten days. Assuming of course that all went well.

This I think is a good time to learn a little more about the *Lalande*. Up to now I have given you some idea of what sort of ship she was in 1948. Personally I have to ask myself, knowing what I know now and this is almost sixty years later, was she really up to sea-going standards. The ship had very little equipment on board, no electronics, apart from the radio room which from time to time was unreliable. No radar and certainly no satellite navigation on board and no telephones for communication between departments. In fact only the barest essentials by today's standards. Mind you, it probably suited the old man who knew nothing else all his life at sea. There was no doubt we had a long way to go. It did seem that there was a strong possibility that the company might well be thinking of getting rid of her on our return to the UK.

Never mind, we were plodding southwards at a steady nine knots and it was fairly obvious by the look on the second mate's face that a satisfactory day's run was being made.

Personally I would rather have not seen his face as there was no love lost between us. He could not wait to give me rotten work to do. Ah well, never mind, I had been warned about this so had to get a grip of myself and rise above it. Our destination was Rio, the jewel of the South Atlantic. The weather was glorious and everybody seemed to be getting along fine. As this was my very first trip I was appointed to the carpenter, another Scot, as my mentor. No one could understand him either. Actually he, like the lamp trimmer, was from Stonaway and both came from a world far away from anything we would ever know. They were marvellous men in their field. The lamp trimmer could splice the thickest of wires and make rope work talk. He made all his own clothes and was always in demand from the bridge or engine room for his sheer knowledge accumulated over a lifetime. However he had an affinity with the drink in no small way when ashore. I never saw him or the carpenter (chippy) ever rebuffed for their shore-based lapses. At sea they were excellent at their jobs and everyone respected these qualities above all else.

However once the gangway was put ashore that was it, straight to the nearest boozer, to be usually found the worst for wear for several days later. I owed all my seamanship to those two, and I consider myself lucky to have sailed with them. How was I to know the importance of having some of these skills over twenty-five years hence when I built a boat to sail single handed across the North Atlantic? I don't know what we would call such men to day, but to us all they were great characters. Probably in the long run, life is full of all sorts of folk, but when you are confined it is a different matter. Literally living cheek by jowl, as for instance where there were twelve living in one cabin it was impossible not to have some outlet. When I think about it I count myself lucky to have been three in a cabin, albeit it was about nine feet square and for a period of up to two years if required. These cramped conditions would never be tolerated today.

Our course would take us east of Fernando de Noronha, nicknamed Devils Island, being a penal settlement, just off the north Brazilian Coast and then continue southwards to Rio. Apparently we would gently lose the coast during this time passing Pernambuco and Bahia on the way. We were informed by the second officer, who all of a sudden seemed keen to expound his own knowledge that we would alter into the coast to pick up Cape Frio, before picking up Rio itself.

What a character

I believe that all of us somewhere in our lives have a very special person to whom we pay homage. I think that in this case, it would have had to be the Captain of the S.S. *Lalande*. Captain 'Polly' Purton was a tiny little man, barely five feet tall, in his mid-sixties with a quiet sense of humour. Who, without a lot of fuss, seemed to me completely in charge. Saying little and not really a mixer we all treated him with the utmost respect. You never saw him without a Park Drive cigarette in his hand and a packet of fifty in his back pocket. This would probably not be approved of today because of the health risk. However his interest was in the running of the ship, which he seemed to do by observing what was happening on board and then by making his feelings known to everyone. Of course he seemed to have an uncanny intuition and to know which person was responsible for any misdemeanour.

I well remember leaving the Thames estuary, when the following morning I was cleaning the brass telegraph with the mandatory sand and water, not Brasso for sure for that would cost money. The "old man" beckoned me over to where he was standing on his box, necessary because he was so short. "Come here, lad," he said to me. Stopping my brass cleaning I obeyed. "Tell me, lad," he said, "Do you know how to navigate?" I remember blurting out that I been to a nautical college in London and that I was now doing a correspondence course. I can see him now looking at me and repeating himself, "Do you know how to navigate?" Then leaving his box he was standing on and coming close to me, he put his finger on the side of his nose and said, "This is what you navigate with, my lad." He then walked off the bridge without a second glance in my direction.

Probably this had some bearing on his behaviour which took place every mid-day after a noon position had been taken by the second and third mates. All of this had been taken by the observation of the sun, using sextants. The two mates, having obtained this position on the chart and after checking everything out, blew down the voice pipe to the old man who would then come up to see the noon position. This was the norm on any ship. As cadets we were expected to learn this.

The old man having appeared on the bridge would draw himself up to his full height and observe the position on the chart. Then without further adieu he pulled a carpenter's pencil from behind his ear and re-plotted the position. Only minutely, I might say, but just sufficiently to show who was boss. He would then be away for a gin and tonic before lunch and an afternoon snooze. The sooner I am Captain, I thought, the better it would be!

Destination Rio

I remember it well. It was very early morning with just the dawn coming up. All night ships had been passing us going in and out from Rio, The old man had ordered a reduced speed. There would not be a berth for us until later in the day, so it was slow ahead. We cadets were now on watch. I was on the eight to twelve am. I had a fantastic view of it all.

We had altered course a little after midnight, to steer for Cape Frio and would do the same when we came abeam of the Cape. This would bring us in line with the harbour some eighty miles away. The first sighting of Rio was the mountain in the distance with this incredible figure of Christ on its pinnacle. This was Corcovado and it almost seemed to touch the clouds. The outline of this amazing harbour started to take shape. Gradually the City of Rio started to emerge. It seemed as if this mountain or enormous hill was covered in small buildings, which turned out to be a shanty town. At the foot of this mountain lay the city of Rio and as we turned in towards the harbour and opened up the land, we could see the famous Sugar Loaf with its aerial railway. Then there was a small but not insignificant airport.

As we approached the mouth of the harbour estuary we turned to starboard and met the swell. Now with Rio to port and the wonderful sight of Niteroi to starboard with its cliffs and some very smart looking properties. We took the pilot on board and went to anchor in the roads. We three cadets were placed on gangway duty to await customs clearance from the office. The only thing 'mail' was all that we lads were waiting for and after a long and anxious wait, I received just one letter. As air mail was so slow, it had obviously come by a passenger liner. Mine was from home with all the nuances one would expect from parents, who were missing their only son and to a great extent was a repeat of everything that had been said to me a few weeks earlier when I said goodbye.

I do remember the postscript written by Dad asking me to give the old man his kindest regards. Not quite the right thing for me to pass on under the circumstances. There was also a p.p.s. stating that mother had not been well, but telling me not to worry. That sort of thing helps life enormously when you are miles away and had no means of communication other than by letter which could take two or three weeks to arrive.

Actually when I did eventually get ashore I went up to the office to find out what the situation would be if it was necessary to get home in an emergency. It was explained to me that I had joined the merchant service and this was one of the drawbacks. However, in extenuating circumstances the office would always do its best to keep one informed through head office. That therefore had to suffice.

What happened next was quite remarkable. Having anchored and the ship cleared by customs, a Shell Mex launch drew alongside the gangway, with someone coming aboard. Within minutes I was called to Mr Spooner's cabin. Knocking at his door I entered to see he had a visitor. Addressing me, Mr Spooner said, "This is Mr Nichols, Chief Engineer with Shell Mex in South America, who, I believe knows a relation of yours." Then Mr Nichols, said, "A distant relation from Quorn Nr Loughborough, a Mr Gibbs, whom I know, has sent me a letter telling me of your presence here in Rio. Mr Spooner has kindly given you leave over the weekend. My wife and I would like you to come and stay." What a total surprise but a very welcome one of course. Now back to my fortunate encounter with Mr Nichols from Shell Mex.

You will not believe this, but I arrived at the Nichol's apartment which overlooked Ipanema beach and it was a most sumptuous apartment. What a spot looking out over the South Atlantic. Anyway, having been introduced to another couple who were also taking of light refreshment, I could not believe my eyes. For on their mantleshelf was a photograph of a girl about my age. I just couldn't help myself and turning to Mrs Nichols and feeling quite confused, I said, "Excuse me, Mrs Nichols, I know this girl, at least I think I do, unless she has a double." "Well," she said, "You well may do so. She lives just outside Shepshed near Loughborough." "That," I said, "is Joanna, I took her out just before I joined the ship." What a small world isn't it?

The days ahead were long and busy and there was night work as well. We lay along the quay which seemed to stretch for ever. A number of the company ships lay alongside, either discharging and going south or loading for the continent and then home. Most of us seemed to be in and out of Liverpool. However our remit was world wide if required. The surprise for me was that one of the company ships that had left that day for the UK had an old school chum of mine from the Grammar school on board. I think he left the Merchant Navy soon afterwards, for I never heard of him again.

Ashore for a few drinks

Now with several company ships together, we lads were able to discuss anything and everything. There were eight of us in all and we had a great time sharing our experiences. One night we all went ashore together and without realising it I was introduced to a drink called kasasha, which is made from wood alcohol, deadly stuff. Before long I was out for the count. I remember waking up the next morning lying on a straw bale on the quayside. I can only assume that I managed to get up the gangway on my own. I don't remember being put under a lifeboat and didn't come round until the following day.

Apparently my pals had given me a glass of water which had the result of making me drunk again. Still we all did it once and no one seemed to be the worst for it. Looking back we all had a great time.

Sitting here now on a rather bleak January day in 2008, I can cast my mind back without difficulty and see this incredible city with its brilliance, its mosaic pavements, wide avenues magnificent buildings, shops and thoroughfares, American cars and first class restaurants.

Today anybody reading this would say, "so what". The advent of television and easy access to flight could make this very boring reading. I think it is well sometimes to recollect that when I first arrived there some sixty years ago, that the integration between cultures was based on who you were and indeed your financial standing in the community. If you were British, you had a certain lifestyle conducive to your social order, often dictated by your position in your work place.

Most jobs were for three years. If you were married you did your first tour, for that is what it was called, without the family, coming home on the mandatory three months' leave after these three years. There was little or no television to whet the appetite. The majority of people who lived there were working for companies. Of course there were the rich elite as had been the case always. All our passengers without exception were either those travelling on business or in exceptional circumstances doing the grand tour. I was to meet one or two of these later.

Back to talking about Rio, this jewel in the east coast of Brazil, I think I have intimated in my initial sighting of the city, that there was definitely two sides to this remarkable city. Rio itself is situated on the coastline with magnificent beaches and offshore islands. Everywhere the growth is prolific and the obvious wealth of flora and fauna incredible. On top of which stood the statue of Christ, probably a hundred foot high, was something I shall never forget. So different from anything I had seen before.

One hears of streets being paved with gold. Well the streets were wide and clean and the pavements on the main thoroughfare were done in mosaic patterns and the shops were fantastic. But as I was soon to find out, there was another side to life. However, with all this apparent opulence there was a certain poverty which I found difficult to understand. Probably this is a result of finding this jewel on the coast with such diverse surroundings

This became totally apparent when one afternoon having acquired some time off, I found myself with one of the engineers of the ship walking the streets to the beach. We decided we would take the road round to the west side of the rock and see what it was like.

We had heard plenty about the shanty town and this meant passing through an area of factory shops where alligator handbags were being made. In fact anything it seemed could be done with an alligator. Another most amazing product was the

making of butterfly trays all laid under glass. My wife and I have one to this day. Beautiful as they were, I was glad to hear that years later these practices all stopped, but that was nothing to what we were to experience as we climbed this incredible mountain road with Christ's figure on the top.

I think it took us a little time to realise what we had walked into for we were amidst the most appalling squalor. The street was full of young and old people pressing their wares onto us. This I might add was the least of our worries, for without exception the poverty was unbelievable. But the glaring thing was that almost without exception many children were crippled. Apparently this was done to them so that they became beggars, particularly the small children, all trying to sell their wares. In all my years since I have never seen the like again. It took us both some time to get over that experience and of course there were brothels every where. Many of the girls were very young, and you only had to look at their eyes to see the damage inflicted. As the trip progressed it became plain to me that I had to grow in my ways and that a broader outlook was necessary to survive Brazil. As far as possible we had to take these people in that context and as was obvious from the discussions that sometimes resulted from our little get-togethers, we had to take each country as we found it.

I, for one found this a help and removed much of the prejudices that I had bottled up inside myself, having been brought up in a very narrow pre-war atmosphere, very worried if you didn't comply. It was quite a revelation to remove much of this thinking. In other words – Bailey, stop being such a know-all and a prejudiced prig.

After that rather exciting encounter, life seemed rather dull on board. But by the weekend, we had completed our discharging and with everything secure prepared to leave for Santos. As money was non-existent, sitting on a hatch in the evening, with hopefully a beer from the steward had to suffice. We were now being pressurised by Mr Spooner as to how far we were on with our studies. This was all set for us, in my case by the nautical college Sir John Cass in Jewry Street just off Tower Hill. This work required weekly attention and in those days was termed a correspondence course, which I did not hold in very high esteem as we never managed to get our papers back in time. Nevertheless I think we all did our best and somehow or other we all managed to pass.

Before we left the following day we were called to Mr Spooner's cabin. Naturally we thought, this was going to be for a good telling off as we had overstayed our welcome at the Seaman's Mission the previous night. The reason we had gone there was we had been informed by the lads off the ship astern, that there was free food but only soft drinks. So we had hot footed it there and at least we didn't have to pay.

We were summoned to hear that the old man thought we cadets should be able to earn some extra cash and that Mr Spooner should sort this out. It would amount to the magnificent sum of one shilling and sixpence an hour to be paid in the currency of the country we were in. We were thrilled and the Chief Steward would sort the job out, the work being anything and everything which needed to be done on a ship like the *Lalande*.

N.º 43   F.1.

ACCOUNT OF WAGES

(Sec. 132, M.S.A. 1894.)

Name of Ship and Official No.

LIVERPOOL
N.T. 1055   N.P. 576

ISSUED BY THE MINISTRY OF TRANSPORT

Name of Seaman	Ref. No. in Agreement	Income Tax Code
...J. BAILY	43	S...

Date Wages began	Date Wages ceased	Total period of Employment	
		Months	Days
...M... Aug		7	21

A. EARNINGS

7 Months at £...per month	52	— —
Days at ...9.5... per day		
Increase of Wages on promotion by £... per month for ...months....days		
Overtime ...hours at ...1.6...per hour	5	10
War Risk Money ...months ...days at £...per month		
TOTAL EARNINGS	67	1 4

DEDUCTIONS

B.	Particulars	Amount
Reduction of Wages, on disrating by £... per month for ...months....days		
Advance on joining		
Allotment		
Forfeitures		
...Pension Fund		
Income Tax		
OTHER CASH ADVANCES, STORES, &c. (in order of date):—		
CASH	52	2 2
	2	6 8
	8	1
NAT INS.	1	
Cash on leaving ship		
Health and Pensions Ins. for ...wks	2	6
Unemployment Insurance for ...wks		11 3
TOTAL DEDUCTIONS		8
Amount Due on day of discharge	1	7

C.

...Leave Due for voyage ...Days	
War Leave Due during Voyage ...Days	
...Leave Still Due Days @ ...per Day	
Subsistence Allowance ...Day @ ...per Day	

LOOK AFTER YOUR MONEY.

When you are paid off, take from the pay table only enough cash for your immediate expenses.

The Ministry of Transport provides the following facilities *free of all charge*; apply to the Superintendent Mercantile Marine Office.

MONEY ORDERS. You can send a Money Order payable to yourself or to any relative or friend at almost any port in the United Kingdom free of cost. This will save you carrying a large sum of money and insures you against loss or robbery.

SAVINGS BANK. Deposit any sum you do not need for immediate expenses in the Seamen's Savings Bank. You can withdraw *free of expense* the whole amount of your deposits at any Port you please, or withdraw portions of your money first at one Port and then at another.

Meanwhile it is earning you interest at the rate of 5d. per month for every £10; it is helping your country and is kept safe for you.

CERTIFICATES

Savings Certificates are obtainable from Post Offices, Banks and Mercantile Marine Offices in the United Kingdom.

They are a British Government Security and provide an easy means of safe investment which is not subject to fluctuation in value. A Certificate costs 15s. and accumulates interest annually which is free of Income Tax. After 5 years the value of a Certificate becomes 17s. 6d., and after 10 years 20s. 6d.

PROMOTION AND DISRATING.

When a Seaman is promoted, or disrated, wages should be calculated for the whole period of the voyage at the rate per month originally fixed and the amount of the increase or decrease, for the period subsequent to the promotion or disrating should then be added or subtracted. The wages for the two parts of the period should not be calculated separately and added together. (See Sec. 59, Merchant Shipping Act, 1906).

55

We leave for Santos

With Santos only a half a day away, we cast off late morning. For me it had been my first foreign port and, as I was to find out before long, the most up-to-date in Brazil. We had been informed of the new capital Brasilia which was started in the thirties being built inland. Actually I never ever saw it but apparently today it is a fine city. One imposing feature which has always stuck in my mind about Rio was an old battleship lying further down the quay, of what vintage I never found out, with the most enormous clock fastened to the mast. It is really funny how certain things stick in your mind.

However much you enjoy ports it always great to feel the ship moving under you again, clean air and a clean ship do wonders for moral, not forgetting time to get a clear head and the added expectations of the next port. We were due in Santos the next day where the last part of the cargo would be discharged. Apparently orders as to what we would be loading was not known. But Liverpool had ordered parts for the boilers to be sent by whatever means to Belem Para in the mouth of the Amazon to await our arrival. So at least we had some idea of our loading route. The following morning we rounded the high hills to starboard and into the narrow entrance to lie alongside in Santos.

Chapter 8

Santos

The Port of Santos, which was little more than a river and at the end of this, mountains towered above and through them was the city of Sao Paulo. Santos itself was little more than a small town with room for very few ships alongside. We turned in the river and in a short space of time it was hatches off and the final discharge. It was then that I had my second very pleasant surprise about my roots.

For there lying in the bottom of the hold some twenty-five feet down was a steel girder which was part of an overhead crane. On it in bold letters was the following 'Morris Cranes, Loughborough'. That brought a bit of an emotional reaction from yours truly, I can assure you, as this was my first time away from home and all that remembering of home was just too much.

So here we were totally discharged, and that to a seaman means one thing – that the ship was lying at its highest point out of the water, fully loaded there can be as much as thirty-two feet under the water. This morning, empty as we were drawing less than twelve feet at the stern and eight feet at the bow. I well remember Mr Spooner, having we three cadets with him while he walked the ship with the bosun, discussing the work to be done.

The big job was the painting of the ship's hull, which the entire deck crew would work on. We were four hundred and sixty feet in length with some nasty overhangs to get round, both on the bow and stern. Of course this is 1948 when there wasn't a safety line in sight and knowing nothing about such things, I actually believe in common sense, or we would say "a bit of savvy". We had fewer problems with sheer stupidity than today, but that is only an old man talking, so forget I even mentioned it.

I think during the week we had laid alongside, I had walked the length and breadth of this small port. We resisted as best we could the 'delights' on offer and we looked forward to the next port. Finally mail was starting to arrive. This was a great boost to morale, at least in most cases. However nothing always seems to be straight forward, and as I found out on subsequent voyages, life can give some nasty blows, especially when you are not expecting it. On this particular delivery, courtesy of the Royal Mail Line ship, one of the engineers had received a letter advising him that his wife had cleared their house out and gone to live with his brother in another town. Not the best sort of news to receive when you are so far away from home and what is worse little chance of any communication in the near future. Anyway it became part of the life on board.

A very upset Captain

Early the next morning it was all hands over the side in the hope of completing the painting the next day. When without realising it, a very trendy boat, similar in size to the *Lalande*, glided past to take up the berth directly ahead. Without doubt, one and all were transfixed at this very smart cargo boat.

From what we could see she was well equipped. No sound emitted as she pulled alongside the quay, no steam from winches. Indeed derricks were already being made ready for lifting the cargo. We ourselves were all puff and blow and noisy. Still painting the ship's hull, we could not believe what we were seeing.

In the late afternoon we three cadets were called to Mr Spooner's cabin to be told that we were to accompany him with the Captain 'Polly' Purton and others. We had been invited to go aboard this rather remarkable vessel that was now lying astern of us.

That evening we went aboard this amazing ship to a 'right royal treat'. The manners, the courtesy and the magnificent spread, the latter being much more of an interest to us cadets was beyond belief.

This ship was Japanese, freshly out of Liverpool, our home port with a speed of 15 knots as opposed to our 9 knots. She had the very latest radar and technology aboard, and all the derricks were electronically operated and what was more, diesel engines. I had not really grasped the significance of all this as I was just enjoying the moment, However, we were eventually marched back to our dear old *Lalande*. What a difference to be seen as we walked up the gangway, when we were ordered up to the old man's "day room".

Standing there in a row all three of us were asked to comment on the inevitable. What we had just witnessed seemed to come from another planet. However, the old man having lit up the woodbine came into his day room. Without doubt he seemed to be troubled and without further adieu addressed us.

"Well, lads," he said, looking agitated, "What did you think of that?" I believe I said, "What a magnificent ship," for want of something better to say. There was then a deathly hush with the old man puffing, "I believe that I was sunk three times during the last war, three times mind you and we won the war. That ship you have just been on board, a ship highly superior to ours, and a Japanese ship at that much faster, with radar and it looks like the latest in everything and is on our run from Liverpool with fine a cargo. All the things we have not gentlemen!" Now sounding very angry the old man finished by saying, "And they lost the war! What do you reckon to that? "

Later that evening Mr Spooner came down to our cabin, which we all felt was very good of him, as none of the three of us had been in the war, to enlighten us as to the situation that the old man had been in. That included him being in the two great wars. The old man had served his time on a square rigger and had been in many a life-threatening situation. What a life it had been, so needless to say I think we all felt very humbled by this experience.

Mr Spooner went on to tell us that old man's father had been a skipper in square-rigged ships in the West Indies' trade. What an adventurous age to have lived in.

In attempting to put on paper the past, it just struck me that irrespective whether anyone ever reads this, it is a way for me to relive those early days. I actually believe that most of us have a great affinity with those far distant times. In thinking that they were better days is where most of us go wrong. How often for instance do we claim the past to be better than the present? Of course, I think life is so much faster today, for better or worse. Why I have gone off at a tangent like this – because I have always felt that the experience I had on this voyage in 1948 was akin to being in a time warp, nothing seemed to have progressed in Europe. That is in comparison to countries like Japan.

The ship apart, we were due to sail the next morning for the Amazon region. As none of us had ever been up there, this was a very exciting prospect.

Chapter 9

Amazon bound

I suppose the obvious heading for this next chapter is excitement, for the very word Amazon, conjures up all sorts of thrilling adventures we lads might well be part of.

The immediate problem for us was being assigned to the engine room for eight hours, i.e. two four-hour shifts on different watches. I was assigned to the 4-8 hour stint which was the 2nd engineer's watch. This was an experience not to be missed as most cadets saw very little of this part of the ship and usually in a very superficial way. We observed only what we were involved in and not without some cost to ourselves as no explanations were ever given to a mere cadet. Fortunately for me Brian, the senior cadet, in his usual zestful way had opened a valve, the wrong one I hasten to add, and scolded himself. Luckily for him the quick action from one of the greasers averted what could have been a disaster.

The Brazilian Coast

Having acquired a very good pair of binoculars from my maternal grandfather on my last trip home, I found the coastline fascinating. Most of it was high and rugged with inlets to small towns and settlements.

I think here I must say that there were very few roads connecting the coastal strip, consequently travel was mostly done by sea. To this end dozens of small passenger ships, with beautiful lines and racked funnel and masts and for the passengers comfort with double awnings to keep the sun off, passed by.

These small delightful boats plied their way up and down the coast. I was informed some time later by a member of the crew, after myself having waxed lyrical over these craft, that I should take a closer look at these boats, before making such remarks. Many of them were in a dreadful state as many had been on the go since the early 1900s and were suffering somewhat as old things are apt to do.

As indeed the *Lalande* was now, with boilers and general ambience in such a bad state of repair. I was told by a crew member of another ship who had been given a lift on one of the coasters that conditions were not what they seemed. I enquired where he had got his information from. He told me he had to join a ship further down the coast. I suspected he had missed the departure of his own vessel, no doubt through his own inability to get back on board. This was nothing unusual, I can assure you. Early the next morning we passed abeam of Rio, where a large Royal Mail Liner was rounding Niteroi on the starboard side of the harbour, the residential side. The whole place looked fabulous and I looked forward to future calls. We now had about 1200 nautical miles to go before Belem and the start of the Amazon.

The busy port of Bahia.

There were only two main ports to pass, that are with harbours and anything like towns. The first was Bahia in the port of San Salvador and the other further up the coast was Pernambuco in the port of Recife.

From then on, I believe I was told we would steam round the North East bulge of Brazil with tiny inlets. This was where we could anchor and load or offload into lighters and barges for their run up the rivers to small towns. This I was really looking forward too. I had heard of these remarkable inlets, where everything was done from the ship as there were no harbours, only barges and lighters to load into. Having to be totally autonomous, this was the real thing, as far as I was concerned. Quite naturally as this was the company run, Lamport & Holt ships were constantly in the area, passing up and down the coast either outward bound or homeward bound.

After the first few days we cadets found that we were so filthy from being down below. To be quite frank with you, none of us had the energy left after each watch in the engine room to have a wash. You must bear in mind that we were getting the sticky end of the job in appalling heat. The gauges showed it to be one hundred and thirty degrees on the middle plates. Having already been informed that it would be one hundred and twenty degrees in the Amazon and what with seventy / eighty degrees and high humidity it did not auger very well for anyone's comfort. What should be explained here is that when the *Lalande* was built in 1920, comforts for crew were a very low priority. We had no air-conditioning on board at all, that included the officer's accommodation, let alone any iced water, which was really a must in that sort of heat.

We had an unexpected call into Fortaleza. It seemed to be the norm to pick up and drop off when passing small ports. Often a launch or company tug would come out and save the difficulties in anchoring, if the sea was at all rough. Actually I was surprised how small Fortaleza was. We dropped our piece of machinery successfully, and continued on up the coast. No doubt one day this would be a thriving town with all the work going on in the harbour mouth. I could visualise that even then.

I was surprised to see how primitive the facilities were. The shore showed huts with straw roofs and as far as I could ascertain no other buildings at all. Let us say shore labourers wore little else but loose clothes, many of them wearing straw hats and sporting pipes. There boss ganger or foreman spoke a little English and I was surprised to hear Mr Spooner getting on so well with the Portuguese language. It does not say much for we Brits who, I soon found out, knew little of other languages. A disgrace I called it and I include myself in this company. I vowed there and then I would do some thing about it, but I am afraid and ashamed to say I never did.

We proceeded further up the coast, heading more or less in a north-west direction. Then we plodded on towards two other small ports. Plodding was the operative word as the boilers were now playing up. We had to reduce our speed down to five knots. Apparently the water in the Amazon can run up to nine knots, and this could well make manoeuvring very difficult.

I can well imagine the old man's concern, as Belem is a good run into the mouth of the river. The town is on the south side of the mouth of the river and I believe the idea was to creep round as close inshore as we could, as we were a light ship with not much cargo at this time. This would also give us the advantage of being able to keep out of the main current. You must remember, as I have already remarked, that in the Amazon the current comes down from the Andes at a rate of nine knots.

This is probably a good time as any to explain the problem the engine room was having with the boilers. As I had been in the engine room and been shown why we were in this predicament my explanation is at least from first hand, as the second engineer had given me the benefit of his expertise.

The *Lalande* was a steam ship. In other words she was driven by steam. The boilers were Scotch boilers as I have already told you. In other words the boilers were round and about ten feet in diameter. They were full of metal tubes, if my memory serves me right, several hundred of them. They contained sea water and when fired turned into steam, which drives the engine.

What happened over the years was that the tubes had corroded and the only way that steam could be kept up was to blank the offending tubes off. This was achieved by inserting stoppers into the offending tubes. It was the arrival of these stoppers which were coming from the UK hopefully via New York, then to Belem, that would allow our progress to continue.

Our trials and tribulations below decks had produced a number of very good buddies. One or two were very obviously keen to show us the seedier side of the ports we were going to enter. I must say this was not something new and was looked upon by some as somewhat of a sporting venture, sometimes with not very pleasant situations evolving. Still sailors will be sailors, and it was not surprising sometimes who took advantage of the situation. Having passed by Recife we were now leaving the more populated coastline for small ports, most of which fed the small towns or settlements upriver.

Another routine day, but a surprise awaited us as we were invited by the second mate to try our hand at taking bearings on points of land. This we felt was in response to some of the earlier chivvying by Mr Spooner who was anxious to see that we lads had something to show for our studies on our return to the UK. We were given an old chart in the chart room, and suitably armed with compasses and dividers, proceeded to chart our way up the coast. We had to identify the coastline for ourselves. This being our first piece of navigation we took it in a serious light and after four hours we were more than gratified to receive favourable remarks from my friend the second mate.

One of the many inlets

The following morning we three were woken up to a shout from the bosun directing the launching of a lifeboat. We had 'heaved to' and were lying about a quarter of a mile offshore. There were no markers for the entrance into the river as this was due to more or less no shipping being there. The lifeboat was sent off to take soundings just to see no silting had taken place and we could steam in to the bay safely, or at least if some silting had taken place, then the most favourable deep water spot could be found.

I was to go along with the third mate and several able seamen and was presented with an oar and a remark to the effect that "We shall now see what you are made of, my lad." All aboard and with the third mate at the helm we pulled for the entrance. As anyone knows that when you are facing the stern when rowing, I never saw the entrance to the bay until we were inside. It was sand as far as you could see, sand on all sides and according to the seaman taking soundings, more than enough water for our requirements. We therefore turned about and made our way back to the ship. With the lifeboat safely in its davit, we proceeded through the unmarked channel. Little by little I felt I was becoming a sailor at last.

With the engines on half speed ahead we entered what to me was something out of this world. Not a soul in sight and perfect peace. What I could not understand was what were we, a 10,000 ton ship, doing here? I was to learn soon enough!

You know in most walks of life, particularly as we were working together, that advanced knowledge of what was happening would have been of some advantage. We seemed, however to have very definite rules of our own and this was not always to our advantage. So lying there in this most ideal spot ignorant or not of the immediate future seemed a little bizarre to say the least. This time the senior cadet, Brian, tackled the mate as to "what the hell we were up too". Mr Spooner, like the trooper he was, realised our ignorance of the present situation and came over with the following explanation.

As there had always been so little roads on the coast, a gentleman's agreement had been set up many years ago. This was that if there were requirements for any settlement upriver mostly coastwise ships would handle it. Paperwork was kept to a minimum as long as the company were not aware or involved. It just made me laugh to think of our 10,000 ton ship stuck in the channel and sending a report through to Liverpool that they were stuck at the entrance to an inlet near Cabedelo whilst delivering a ton of potatoes. Mind you, whilst we were there a small launch came downriver and what was put over the side was tools and medical supplies. The next morning, I heard that the old mans drink's cupboard was well stocked. Good for him I thought. Perhaps I can do the same thing myself one day,

We proceeded up the coast at a reduced speed after a nerve-racking departure after what had been a wonderful day anchored in a bay in this remote part of North Brazil. Before I go any further I have a most unusual story to tell you.

Six of us, under the guidance of the third officer, had a chance to explore in the afternoon and, after having rowed across to the nearest point, we anchored in six feet and then swam ashore. Walking over the sand we encountered miles of dunes, which were actually hidden from the ship. No doubt if we had taken the trouble to climb the mast we would have seen so much more.

To our utter surprise there in the middle of nowhere was a tiny church. By the way, we were all sober. The church had a cross above the door making no mistake what it was and below it, behind one of the other dunes was a village of about a dozen huts, all of which had straw roofs. There was the odd tethered goat and dogs ambling about, but some instinct told us to not go inside. We saw one or two people walking nearby but that was all. The third mate was most emphatic that we should leave.

However my curiosity got the better of me, I slid across the dune and not being able to help myself tried the door to the church. It was open and it was a remarkable sight. Having so little time to take it all in, I imagined the church might hold a dozen people. No seats as such, an altar and what was most outstanding, were the receptacles on the altar which appeared to be gold colour. I have to now confess that ever since that day I have said these objects were gold. However on reflection it seems highly unlikely. Probably they were more likely brass, I think. It had been a lovely dream of mine to believe that it was gold. Still we are all allowed a little licence sometimes in our lives. That then is goodbye to this part of the world. I wonder what it looks like today. Having just been with my wife on a cruise off the Venezuela coast and calling at the San Blas Islands, the Indian huts reminded me of this village.

We proceeded again at a reduced speed after yet another upset in the engine room which we were all getting used to by now. It was to be hoped when we reached Belem our spare parts had arrived from England via New York. The real problem, as explained to us by the chief engineer, was that the boilers in the ship were Scott's boilers. This caused a bit of good humour amongst the Liverpuddlians aboard but as we all really knew it was because the boiler tubes were completely worn out.

As the chief engineer once again tried to explain this to the old man, who to be fair was on his last trip and I suspect, his only real thought was to get home as quickly as possibly and in one piece. His attitude was that it had gone well for twenty-seven years so why not now. It did not seem an unfair assessment on his part.

However the plan was to get to Belem where the offending boiler could be mended. The distance we had to cover would take about four or five days which was just one more problem.

Like any journey at sea, time is spent watch keeping and preparing for the work the ship will have to do in port. In the majority of ports everything was on hand as the delay of a ship in port meant a loss of profit called demurrage. I will give a brief explanation.

The schedule for ships alongside was always tight. Not forgetting that many came from half way across the world to deliver cargoes. Many of the quayside cranes were from home and if I ever felt a bit homesick I would walk along the quay and look at the names Stodart and Pitt, made in Bath, England, on the side of the numerous cranes.

These were all hydraulic and would not do today, I'm sure! But nevertheless they never failed. As a way of introducing you to North Brazil and the Amazon I will attempt to give a little of the shipping background. Not a history lesson as such, but what effect the region had on shipping from the time when Lamport & Holt first did the coast and rivers in the early twentieth century. It was a truly remarkable enterprise.

Chapter 10

Lamport & Holt Line's early days

Those entrepreneurs, for that is what these shipping magnets were, had seen the making of the company with the transportation of the rubber trees from the Amazon to Malaya. Quite simply Malaya had better climate conditions for these trees to flourish. These were very astute gentlemen who built up a fleet starting with sail and steam engines. This allowed them to get up rivers also sailing to the West Indies and so increasing their trade. This was a massive continent stretching far across to the Andes, the majority of which was uninhabited and was indeed a chance to help develop such a continent.

By this time the company was growing rapidly, building new ships to take to the Argentine right down to Cape Horn. Small ships were sold off and bigger and better ships, which were faster, had taken their place. At one time the company owned over sixty ships, a mighty fleet and with it came power and standing in the shipping world.

But as is often the case having had Two World Wars, this took their toll. It was reckoned that in the Second World War alone up to sixty per cent of the ships were lost. This did not preclude the company going world wide, as before the war. Some wonderful passenger ships had been built feeding the then early tourist trade to the States and Far East. These were first class voyages, such as the one I went on, on the *Brittanic* as a passenger, to go as third officer on the *Jutahy* in 1950. However, many books have been written about those times so I will not enlarge on this. Now back to reality.

The North Brazilian coast we were now on was so vastly different from down south, it was like moving into a barren waste land and the nautical reference books like the *Nautical Almanac* certainly didn't go over the top with regard to showing us clarity reference the coast line. We were pleased to note that the second mate was at last showing some interest in our chart work and we quickly found out that a little flattery from us paid dividends.

One evening the old man came up as we were struggling at a much reduced speed. I suspect with time on his hands he went below and returned with weather maps showing us the weather chart for the next six hours. There would be a number of ships on station in the North Atlantic he told us as he puffed on his woodbine. This was where actual weather ships were on station on different parts of the North Atlantic, British, American and French and also other nationalities. Captain Purton was a pleasant old boy, and not adverse to a few jokes when he felt like it. Anyway we were now closing the river fast. The actual mouth is made up of many islands and ships coming from the north enter from the north side and vice versa from the south. It is indeed a wild spot with fresh water running far out into the ocean some two hundred miles. This tells you the strength of the river flowing sea-ward.

Belem (Para) and the Amazon

Belem itself lies on the southern shore and we were told that once everything quietened down the ship would have to be ready on arrival to shut down completely. Except for an auxiliary engine ready to take over whilst the boilers were repaired. Apparently there was a Lloyd's surveyor in the area. He was somewhere upriver and it could be days before he could get to us. So it was planned to strip part of the derricks down and replace wires ready for our loading of timber further upriver. Oporto, Portugal was to be our destination after that.

Spear Fishing – a regular sight

As we turned more into the estuary the sheer magnificence of the shore line grew and small clusters of huts became clearer. Dozens of primitive craft could be seen with one or two people fishing. As the day progressed and the closing of the shore the heat increased tremendously. What was startling was the level of humidity. Two of our crew had already developed boils on their arms. To put it mildly it was not really conducive for the rest of us in these circumstances.

We never had a doctor on board. Only if we were carrying more than thirty-eight passengers, then it was necessary. Consequently all we had was a medical almanac. A sort of 'do it yourself' remedy but the obvious course was to seek medical advice whenever possible. However if there was an accident, what were we to do in an emergency? With a limited amount of equipment on board if you were on a long sea voyage it must be very difficult. Only basic lifesaving equipment was on board. I assumed, with tongue in cheek, that if this was the case the second mate who fancied himself as a bit of a medic might come to the rescue. It was felt by the Company that we had an adequate amount of books and anti-biotics to treat those who indulged themselves with the ladies ashore and that was all we carried. How well I remember that one of my jobs later on when I became second mate, was to administer injections. Obviously this was only after visits to the shore clinics so life was never dull as you can imagine.

Orders came through in that late afternoon as it was just getting dark. Remember that on the line or near enough, it is more or less equal day and night and so with a suitable spot out of the way of traffic we anchored. With anchor watches set we were free to do as we pleased.

The one snag as far as we lads were concerned was that we were unable to nip ashore and of course there was no mail. As I mentioned earlier, a deal had been done with Mr Spooner that we could go on to one shilling and sixpence an hour on overtime. Believe it or not on the way up from Santos, we had made the most of it. If I remember rightly I had about three pounds and in Brazil, believe me, you could go along way on three pounds.

The next morning a boat came alongside with our orders. However, the surveyor had not appeared and as time was pressing, reference our repairs, a spot had been found for us further down the quay. This enabled the engine room to prepare for the surveyor's arrival for as yet he had not yet been found.

This was great news for us as, with luck, we would be ashore that night. The news from home was not that good. Mother had still not recovered from her illness and Dad had written they were going to have a few days at Skegness. This was where mother "could breathe the ozone". She was a great "ozone breather" and more than once I had been hauled in to partake of this myself. I felt that she would approve of the amount of fresh air I was getting in my life on board.

The next morning a company tug with the black, white and blue funnel took our bow line and, not without some false starts, put us alongside in Belem. The pleasant surprise as far as we lads were concerned was that one of Maggie Booth's boats was lying ahead. This was only a small company and it was very smart and up-to-date with its distinctive black funnel. Certainly not of our vintage, so hopefully with a bit of luck and shore leave granted we well might join forces that night ashore.

A sudden urgency descended on the ship, or so it seemed. The main boiler was now shut down. This meant there was only the auxiliary generator to supply lighting and the day-to-day running of the ship. A small lighter came alongside with everything required to repair the boilers. It indeed was a very busy scene. Naughty as it may seem we young cadets were only interested to get ashore for the night.

The most surprising thing to me was that the senior officials were all dressed up to the hilt. The British Consul wore a morning coat, stripped trousers, wing cravat, in temperatures which exceeded one hundred and twenty degrees with a humidity that was very oppressive. Anyway we lads had a couple of nights ashore until the money ran out and then it was staying on board. Belem was like most of these northern ports, very poor and apart from the sort of business area, had nothing to show for itself. I certainly was not impressed.

Towards the end of the week the boiler had generally been repaired with the stoppers that had been sent out. However it did mean that without the full use of the boilers we were without a full head of steam, this would take us up to the island of Jararaca. This I learned means the island of the snakes. There we would load timber for Oporto, in Portugal our next port of call.

With the work done and the ship "made ready", as the old man would say, we cast off the following morning. I was glad to get away from the stifling heat and humidity which was awful. We soon left Belem astern and the promised chance of a cooler breeze we soon realised was somewhat of a myth. Luckily for me I was posted to the bow with strict instructions to keep a look out for small craft passing across our bows. This was the approach into the entrance of this mighty river, the mouth of the Amazon.

I would never forget later that day as the river narrowed, small settlements could be seen ashore with their straw roofs and the cattle penned up actually in the water. This was to keep them safe and of course, from wandering and from predators. We seemed to be somewhat out of the main channel. The river was deep in places with the jungle down to the water's edge.

Jararaca – Island of the snakes

What a beautiful and isolated spot this was and with only the eyes and ears of the bridge to find the island, I seem to have no recollection of seeing it appear. I appreciate it was sixty years ago and one's memory fades. All I do remember was coming on deck because the whistle had been blown and seeing a sky full of incredible birds of all colours. How could they have managed to find the island without me? Very easily I should imagine! Anyway, the fact that I cannot recollect this manoeuvring and the tying up the ropes, nor for that matter the gangway being placed in position amongst the undergrowth, rather baffles me.

But what I do remember was seeing my friend, the second mate, going down the gangway with his rifle, obviously for some sport. He was called back by Mr Spooner and reprimanded in front of the whole ship's company as he returned up the gangway. It actually did a lot of good as the settlement where the native shore gang lived along with their families could have been in danger. Quite right of old Spooner to pull the second mate up. We of course loved this.

We cadets were, as the rest of the crew, subject to the rules of the ship and could not just wander ashore. In the most unusual circumstances we were tied up literally to trees. That is the *Lalande*, not we lads! Out of the main river and with no contact with the outside world, except when the wireless operator, otherwise known as Sparky, was able to make contact. This was very spasmodic due to the close contact of the jungle around us.

Let me explain why we were in this predicament in the first place. We were loading a single assignment of timber, much of it from the shore side. As there were literally no roads on the island the trees were either felled on the other side or I suspect from neighbouring areas. Then they were floated down to us and put aboard by derricks from the riverside. These islanders lived in total isolation of the rest of world and earned their keep by felling trees. When sufficient were ready, the agents downriver would be advised by tug boat and a cargo made up. In this case it was thirty to forty foot logs for Oporto in Portugal. I presumed that they were to be made into wine or beer barrels when they arrived there.

Most timber was hand felled. The only mechanical help they had was an ancient saw, powered by wood chippings in an old steam boiler many years old. The rest was done by hand, the logs from the far side of the island were put in the river and tied into rafts and then guided round to the ship. Then they were tied up alongside ready to be hauled aboard. The ones on the shore side had to be dragged across the island and the men had laid poles long ways so that logs could be dragged easily to the side of the ship.

From what I could see the village or settlement was made up of dwellings set about three feet high, with a wooden floor and straw roof. I do not recollect seeing any women folk there.

All by hand!

After some rather anxious moments moving the ship one way and then the other, we made sure we were lying where the deepest water was to be found. For although there is not a large rise and fall of water in these parts, it was imperative when we had finished loading that we were able to leave with sufficient water under our keel. In this very remote spot there are no tugs, at least tugs capable of moving us or there to help a ship in trouble and needing a pull off the mud.

Every day a small cluster of canoes and battered old boats with rather dubious characters on board would appear alongside, with the obvious intention of plying us with their goods. I was to find this to be the norm in many parts of the world. In this case it was mostly just things to eat, coconut and other exotic fruits.

We were advised not to partake in any of this as the local hospital was back in Belem. I have to say now on looking back it was a wonderful experience to see these islanders and how remote they were from the outside world and their ability to cope and survive. For whilst trying to sell or bargain with us there would be a sudden shout. Then to see a spear or bow and arrow picked from the bottom of the dugout and in the next second a bird or fish killed was spectacular. This would be one of their few meat dishes they would ever eat.

One evening we went ashore after working ship and were invited to a feast by the native people. Bearing in mind that a ship only called about every eight weeks we three lads, the second mate plus a number of the other crew threw ourselves into the event. As there was little else to do it provided some diversion. To sit round an open fire on an island in the Amazon with some of the indigenous people wearing only loin clothes is a vivid memory for me. On a sweltering night with the moon shinning through the trees and out of sight of the ship I had only ever seen such a sight in a Hollywood film before this moment.

It is possibly the one time in my memory that has never been repeated. Whether we quite saw it like that then, is doubtful. All the food was being cooked either on sticks or in some sort of shells. We did not know what most of it was but it was not quite to our taste. However after a few gulps of wood alcohol we became more amenable to our hosts' offerings.

The final scenario was disaster. Brian, the senior cadet spent the night where he flaked out on the floor of the jungle and was only returned to the ship the next morning by one of the islanders. The rest of us somehow or other returned on board. How I shall never know. Most of us were in a terrible state the next morning and given a right rollicking by Mr Spooner, who found himself minus half his crew.

If that was not sufficient problems for the old man, who rather seemed to have gone to ground, I must leave it to the reader's imagination. What I mean by this, Mr Spooner had the ultimate decision to make regarding the inefficiency of the boilers. The state of the one remaining boiler, which had not as yet received the new tubes, was caput. Apparently the new ones should be waiting for us on our return to Belem. We were in serious trouble and leaking dangerously.

The Chief Engineer, having made this known to the old man, gave him a final warning as to the state of play. Right or wrong it was decided to load as much as we could, so work carried on apace. The final straw was that that the intense heat and boiler trouble, which made the generator work very intermittently, had caused the one big freezer we had on board to fail. Consequently, we were ordered to close and seal the freezer off for the moment.

From what I could glean, neither the bridge nor the engine room were happy with the situation. This of course was 1948, when health and safety regulations were something for the future. After all the *Lalande* had been travelling the high seas since 1920, without so much as air-conditioning, mosquito nets, and certainly no refrigeration to put a cool drink in. At the moment we were in a temperature of 120 degrees and 90 degrees humidity, with no chance whatsoever of any relief. The cabins were small and probably what was worse was the fact that the galley, which was something else for heat, was out of bounds. So that was that.

You could ask yourself, why we didn't get out of this place and back to Belem as quickly as possible. What on earth was I doing there? Loading was continuing very slowly from the shore side. Then the surprise came the next morning to find that we were to start loading from the riverside. All morning these enormous logs were being tied up on the river side and were being attached by slings by the natives, who were doing this swimming in the water. I think this next part deserves a separate paragraph at least. I think everyone has at some time or other heard of the life from early explorers' writings.

Chapter 11

No longer a 'Hidden World'

The Alligators, the incredible bird life, with all their wonderful plumage and the most dreaded of all because of their vicious teeth, millions of piranhas. With a body no more than six inches long, but a mouth almost as big as a human being, it was said that if one of us fell over the side and if they smelt blood we would have no chance of survival. They would descend on you in their thousands and there would be very little left in no time at all. We spent quite a time in the evenings throwing the afters from supper into the water just to prove the point.

Then there were the alligators usually seen lying on the banks or just cruising down the river, I suspect waiting for a cadet to fall over board.

The number of times during my attempt to put down the events that happened during 1947/48 on my initial trip on the cargo boat *Lalande*, seems to wane into insignificance, realising as I do that the television can in one night project all that I ever saw or did during that time. I feel that these travel programmes are some of the wonders that television brings into our lives today.

That really nothing is unusual any more and that for someone who is only trying to project those days the whole thing becomes an irrelevance. But I must not dwell on my own inadequacies. What I should be saying is how wonderful the modern world is with its ability to find out about everything and relate by the Internet so readily. Perhaps some of our grandchildren will go into outer space and be just as mesmerised. I hope that they do.

The agent had made arrangements for us to return to Belem and then for a quick getaway as we were already running late before we had even started up the river for Jararaca. We were about to have far more serious problems. The fridge which had had to be sealed off was something that had to be tackled. You can only imagine what the smell was like. The only thing to do was to throw the contents overboard. This need arose because a number of us were being affected, or so it was thought, by the food situation and the smell from the fridge, even though it was sealed. I had by this time an armful of boils looking like fried eggs. To top it all my asthma was acute. To do this we had to alleviate any further problems. A plan of campaign was conceived to get rid of the rotting food at once. All loading of the ship was stopped from the riverside and with face masks at the ready and all doors and portholes sealed the fridge was opened. After a while, how long I do not remember, those brave volunteers went in and emptied the entire contents over the side. They gave our fishy friends one of the finest feasts they undoubtedly had ever had. We all swore we would never ever go for a paddle in this vicinity.

As yet we had not quite completed our catastrophic time on the Island of Jararaca. For on the final day of loading one of the lumbermen who was down below stacking these enormous logs, had his arm crushed when the end of a log trapped him against one of the steel ribs of the ship's side.

How this happened goodness knows but the only consolation was that we were leaving for Belem the following morning. It just shows how ill equipped we were for such an accident. Our first aid kit would be a disgrace today. Luckily there was morphine in the kit, but very little advice as to how to use it, anyway.

A small cabin was cleared and the injured man, probably middle aged was settled in this cabin. The 2nd mate rather fancied his chances as a doctor. However after consultation, I only know about these events, as I had offered to be of assistance. Mr Spooner, confirming with the old man of course, decided that they should do nothing to make matters worse. The morphine seemed to quieten him down and we three lads did a two hour's stint watching over him. Our only orders were to gently release the tourniquet frequently and naturally we did as we were told.

Back to Belem

In the early hours of the next morning we were underway and once we had cleared the jungle properly, Sparky was able to contact Belem and inform the agent urgently of the plight of the injured man. The reply came back within the hour, to do nothing but to keep him comfortable. So ended an experience we lads would certainly not forget in a hurry. Roughly half the crew were suffering either from some type of food poisoning, boils or related complaints. Luckily we would soon be in Belem where medical attention was available. We were all relieved when we got treatment, especially the injured lumberman.

Our stay in Belem was confined to repairing the boilers as more new tubes had arrived from England via New York, sorting the fridge out and general inspection of rigging and anything applicable to safety. Each morning we were marched to the small hospital, for what was called general repairs to the crew who had many nasty boils, cuts and one poor chap had a very nasty gash.

Chapter 12

We set sail for Oporto

I had a problem with my arms and boils but even before we left Belem for Oporto I felt a little easier. I believe I had seven boils altogether. Anyway with medicine and attention from the nurses I became almost human again. We eventually said our goodbyes and wended our way down the Amazon and out into the deep blue sea and a cool breeze. What with feeling better in myself and mail from home informing me of mother's recovery also sailing in the right direction, homeward bound, things were beginning to look up.

Other ships were passing to the south and two of Lamport & Holt ships flashed us during the night wishing us Bon Voyage. Work was progressing well and for once the mood on board lightened.

A typical Amazon inlet.

We were all aware that the old man had not been in evidence for the last few days. Mr Spooner confirmed that he had gout. He explained to one young upstart of an engineer who had had the audacity to suggest that it was time "Polly Purton packed his job in" that the old man had been at sea continuously for fifty-five years. Also that he had first sailed under canvas in square riggers and had been in two world wars and torpedoed twice. These facts given by Spooner had the desired effects with the young engineer beating a hasty retreat.

The rest of the run into Oporto went without mishap, discharging the relevant cargo and with explicit orders to proceed to Antwerp. We set sail on the last leg of certainly an adventurous voyage. Of course to be fair this had been my first trip and I had nothing really to compare it with, I felt a strange sense of euphoria especially as there were no further problems ahead. England and home were a lot nearer and that was impossible to evaluate.

Chapter 13

Antwerp bound

Watches were set and to my relief I was posted to the 8-12 watch which meant I could get all the practice I liked at navigation. In fact the third mate really kept me at it, taking bearings on lights ashore, reporting all ships. After a hectic hour or so he would say, "Come on, Bailey, time for tea." I would brew up in the chart room, then the wonderful moments came when we both stood on the wing of the bridge, mugs in hand discussing the ship's progress and what would we be seeing shortly.

He would answer anything I asked him. Quite frankly I owed him a lot for he certainly gave me that confidence which I found in the next couple of years. This was so vitally important to someone who previously had had little success.

He himself had actually come up from the foc's'le. This meant that he had approached the nearest seaman's office in a sea port and applied for a job as a deck hand. After the first interview to establish that he wished to join, he was then given a test for literacy and practical ability. Assuming he then wished to carry on he was then sent to a training centre. In the case of my friend this had happened just prior to the war and very likely with the recruiting drive being stepped up things may have been hurried through.

Anyway, he obviously passed through the tests and was assigned to a ship through the pool but not a very savoury one at that, I was told. Still I could talk especially to him with all the problems we had on the *Lalande* 'bless her cotton socks'. I have to say with all the ships I sailed on it is she alone who I remember the most.

A great guy

Anyway back to my friend the third mate, not for him a cabin amidships, not that ours was anything to shout about, but the foc's'le aft with all the deck hands. He had come through the ranks but never forgotten his roots.

In the case of my friend he did four years in the foc's'le rising to AB in which time he did correspondence courses. Then he sat an exam for his 2nd mate's certificate, a great achievement for which we all admired him very much.

Brave men

Very many twists of fate happened in the war and I was always fascinated to hear these stories, which often had to be dug out of reluctant heroes. For instance, the bosun a single man who had faithfully served Lamport & Holt for years, was on a ship where the entire bridge personal were wiped out in the Atlantic. He safely brought the ship home to Liverpool and they were great guys. In many cases they used common sense and an extraordinary amount of courage in these times of war.

The English Channel

Two days after leaving Oporto and having had a very fair run through the bay, in the early morning we picked the light up on Ushant to round into the English Channel. So we now had England on our port side and it indeed was a great feeling to know there was nothing between us and home. However there were other pressing problems ahead because of the amount of shipping in the channel, and we cadets continued our watches in the open in the bow with specific instructions to report anything we saw.

In the absence of telephones on the ship we had to indicate any object whatsoever or light by means of the tube which you blew into with the hope that this would be heard on the bridge. This was not always satisfactory. More than once I was given a raspberry from the bridge for mistaking what I saw. I thought if my dad had been there he well might have said something derogatory about the kind of language used. Then on the other hand I doubt it as after all it was called 'character building'.

Guernsey came and went and traffic increased as the channel narrowed. Even then in 1948 there was still a great deal of naval presence, destroyers flying here and there. All of which had the red duster which had to be lowered as they were naval ships and as a sign of respect to our King. Of course cross channel ferries were now operating again but we never saw anything in the pleasure craft line at all. Later that night we could see the lights off Hastings and, as the channel narrowed, the lights of Dungeness where we started to close the French coast to round Cape Gris Nez and then up past Calais to start the run up to Flushing.

We had been notified that we well may have to anchor short of Flushing as there was no night traffic due to the amount of ships still sunk in the river. I believe we reduced speed to try and correct our time of arrival but anyway it didn't work out and we had to anchor up the river to Antwerp. Lucky for me as I would have more time once alongside to meet Dad's Belgian school friend Henri von de Capel.

The approach to Flushing at the mouth of the Schelde was indeed something that we three lads had been looking forward too, as it had been all sea for long enough. Not that the bridge had indicated to us much information really at any time. After all, we did as we were told. Something today which I find myself at logger heads with young people, but that is my problem.

Up the Schelde.

Arriving at Flushing to see the amount of shipping at anchor seemed to indicate possibly a long wait. We were aware that the lock gates at Antwerp had been blown off and that this would indicate a much longer wait than had first been anticipated. We would have to arrive upriver, ready to go in when the height of tide was right.

The next morning, with a pilot and two tugs in attendance, we slowly ventured up the Schelde. The river is very meandering, winding along with a mind of its own. It reminded me of Kenneth Graham's *Wind in the Willows*, a book I had read a thousand times with Ratty and Moley and Toady up to all their tricks.

The duty of cadets was to take watch and watch about for two hours at a time keeping an eye open for anything that might hamper our progress. We saw this as rather a joke as the river still had a number of vessels, or parts of vessels obscuring the main channel. One had only its masts and funnel showing, all sunk one way or another during the war.

Anyway, after a somewhat hazardous few hours, we arrived at the entrance to be in time to enter the dock with sufficient water to get us alongside and tie up. Within the hour we were firmly on the bottom and well secure.

Mail arrived which was what we all wanted, as for some reason during the rest of the voyage we had fared rather badly. Some mail had even been forwarded on from Rio and so there was plenty to catch up on. The problems with mail is where there is no means of reply by a letter back; for instance a letter might arrive with problems, it might be to do with married life, some with money problems, and some with just a short note to say that the wife had gone off with the milkman. Not easy to handle if you are away and no chance of getting home to sort things out. Of course the simple answer was 'do not marry a sailor'.

Rather than bore you with all our ailments acquired in Brazil, I speak of boils, with a capital B. I thought if we tried to forget them, they might disappear. Unfortunately or rather fortunately for those afflicted, we were sent to the local surgery for attendance. In all, between a dozen or so, we could boast about fifty boils. This we ascertained whilst walking to the surgery about a mile away. Much jest was made of who was to be the first victim.

Bearing in mind that Antwerp was still very much in a state, with buildings still bombed and streets looking like building sites, to find the surgery even with the instructions given wasn't easy. Twice the 3rd officer, who was accompanying us, had to return to a previous street to rescue some poor thirsty souls out of the local.

Anyway back to Father's letter, which arrived with the latest mail. Apparently Dad, on hearing that we might be going to the continent for repairs, had contacted the Liverpool office to find if we were indeed going to Antwerp, I will explain. Dad like his father and grandfather went to Loughborough Grammar

School as a day boy as they all lived close to the school. At the beginning of the First World War in 1914, a certain Henri Van de Capel was sent to England by his parents to board at the same school. During his time there he made friends with Dad. I don't believe that a lot of contact was maintained after they left school, probably an occasional Xmas card, but nothing else, Dad had then spoken to the office in Liverpool to confirm our arrival and he had then written to Henri of any likelihood of me meeting up with him. Having approached Mr Spooner with this request he kindly allowed me to go, providing I was back for midday on the Monday. Thinking back now I wonder how on earth we ever managed to co-ordinate anything.

Anyway the plan was set. I had to get myself to Charleroi, where Henri and his family lived, on a certain train changing at Brussels. On arrival at Charleroi there waiting would be Henri's wife with an English newspaper under her arm, to identify herself.

So the following weekend, armed with a sense of anticipation and a scrap of paper with details from Henri indicating my route, I joined the train in Antwerp changing at Brussels for my destination.

After a somewhat uncomfortable ride, having to stand all the way, I was more than pleased to see Madame standing on the station with that wonderful English newspaper under her arm. After a few pleasantries to which we were confined, neither of us being conversant with the other's language, the two of us arm-in-arm marched out of the station.

It is remarkable to think that, after all those years ago and probably I should be forgiven, but for the life of me I find that the recall at this particular juncture some what hazy. I certainly remember Madame. The shabbiness of the clothes she wore was sufficient for me to realise the deprivation these people had suffered. However I cannot remember the streets we were walking through. Anyway it matters not, for before long we stood before one of those lovely Belgium houses. It was a three-storey affair with a lovely decorative front. The door flew open and a very large man grinning from ear to ear grabbed me. "Welcome, Jim, lovely to see you. Do come in." The rest of the day was spent eating and drinking in this obviously lovely old house, but the ravages of war had taken their toll.

He was a great guy and gave me all the gossip on the old days at the Grammar School. I rather suspected he thought Dad to have been a bit of a waster at school so obviously that must be where I got it from.

I had remembered Dad's remarks some years previously about Henri calling him this 'fire eating jovial man'. He then told me he was in the Belgium Government, apparently as a minister.

That evening as we sat having a great time and being introduced to some rather awful wine he became rather serious and literally looking very sad he said to me, "I have to say I have given a great deal of thought to what I am about to say, as you were only a lad during the occupation. But many terrible things happened here as you are aware. We were invaded during the war and I see no reason why you should not be at least familiar with what took place in our country. I wish, with your permission, to show you what some people will do to others. You don't have to of course, but later on you might well wish you had experienced some of this information."

Henri then went on to say that during the war many ordinary people were co-opted to do work for the resistance and amongst these was quite unexpectedly his own mother. I had seen her as we arrived. It was merely a glimpse, but from what I saw she was a lady probably in her late sixties who seemed a very private person. She became involved in the underground movement unbeknown to anyone. Her actual demeanour was apparently suited to the roll she would undertake. It was in the latter part of the occupation that his mother was caught by the Germans and tortured. Suffice to say the war ended and

Madame was freed. This was a very lucky break as many of her fellow Resistance workers were exterminated. The following day I left after a wonderful invigorating weekend and wiser for my talk with Henri. I had the great privilege to say goodbye to his mother by shaking her hand. What a brave lady to be sure.

Arriving back on board I was somewhat surprised to see so much of the engine room all over the deck. The engineers, along with the shore staff had discovered further problems with the boiler tubes. We were to be examined by Lloyds once again and were now waiting a full inspection.

Having given more than enough time and space to the ship's engine, I will conclude by saying that the following week all was sorted and we sailed an hour before high water. The reason for this was that we were aground most of the time due to the lock gate still being out of commission so we had to take advantage of the tide to give us sufficient water to float and to sail away. Of course it was impossible to leave without a final hitch.

As the engines were put slow astern a much decomposed body was thrown up by the propeller, not an unusual occurrence in those days. Obviously the aftermath of the war was producing much of this sort of thing every day.

We proceeded slowly out of the dock, now on full tide and picked our way down the river. We dropped the pilot off at Flushing. After another slow run down, due to the problems in the river and with everything stowed and watches set full ahead on the engine we set course for Liverpool.

The run round was without any further mishaps and after being paid off in Liverpool, the magnificent sum of seven pounds ten shillings a month I might add, I caught the early morning train for Loughborough and couple of weeks' leave. I am sure you can imagine the rest.

As we cadets were always being transferred to other vessels depending on availability, this was obviously an excellent way for us to gain experience especially if a trip had been a long one. The articles we signed on joining allowed the ship to ply the world for up to two years without relieving the crew. However if the ship came back to Great Britain it was normal to pay the crew off, but not always in its home port.

In our case it was Liverpool. This was obviously cheaper for the company, as it was our home port but if we were paid off away from our home port then the company paid our passage home. We had been away seven months, long enough for a descent leave, but we were not told what ship we would join after that.

So it was on the eleventh of June 1948 that I boarded a local train for Lougborough, changing at Manchester with all my worldly goods and the obligatory presents I had purchased on the Brazilian coast. During that first trip I bought all sorts of things from wonderful butterfly trays to bone pottery. We still have most of it now. Today the indiscriminate killing of such beautiful butterflies would not be allowed and I am pleased about that.

I have to laugh to myself when I think of Dad at Loughborough station, when I found that the Austin 12, the pride of the Bailey family, was out of commission, for reasons best known to the garage. It was not an easy job to put right. Consequently in his wisdom Dad had arranged for my trunk to be left at the station and we would walk home, as he said it was only a couple of miles. Mother was waiting anxiously to see me with my favourite meal. I must say I felt that this a bit mean of Dad not to have a taxi. Still knowing him it was not unexpected. Anyway, the next day I was reunited with my trunk and I settled down to some home comforts.

Sitting here in my wooden shed, which I proudly claim to be my office in mid September 2008, I can see clearly back to that day when I arrived back at home to be greeted by Mum and something wet up my trouser leg. For in my absence a dog had been acquired, a little terrier, or that is what we assumed he was, called Binks. This was changed to Binky doo widdle, due to his habit of preferring the dining room carpet instead of the garden. This was due to the fact my mother, always aware he might get out and bark at the neighbours, kept him firmly under lock and key. The snag was that mother, bless her, was very forgetful, something we all learnt to live with. Now at the ripe old age of seventy-eight my lovely wife is having to put up with me.

Consequently if Binks did get out he made the most of it. Twice that I can remember he was taken into the police station, so in his own way he became quite a character. But could you blame him. They always gave him a good meal in the police station so probably that was the incentive he needed.

We actually then lived at the end of the old town. Today there is a ring road which splits where we lived from the new part of Loughborough, the building of which had to be abandoned as war approached.

Back to my Youth

However there were plenty of fields about and, best of all, orchards. One day my pal and I were picking apples in Dr Blackam's orchard when Sgt Dowarty caught me up a tree. My pal escaped but I unfortunately was caught and given, as they said in those days, a good tanning, which I expected. However, on reporting this to Dad, far from giving me another, which was common enough then, he just gave me a good talking to, sent me to my bedroom for a very early night, with no radio, television or play station, however I did have Kenneth William's book *Wind in the Willows*. A book I have never forgotten as Ratty said to Mole, "There's nothing, simply nothing like messing about in boats."

From about 1938 to 1943, certainly when I was around the age of thirteen, we used to have a number of pals, most of whom had brothers or sisters and often fathers who were called up and so the streets were very quiet. Only cars on special duty were out as petrol was severely rationed and only people on essential business, with high priority jobs were allowed petrol coupons. Consequently those few families that had a car and no chance of any coupons, jacked their cars up on bricks for the duration of the war.

So with the streets almost clear of traffic, it became an ideal safe place to play with our home-made trolleys, the wheels coming from old prams and the like.

Several of my friends had relatives who returned from the war zone with hair-raising stories and many nights we lads would sit open-mouthed listening to stories beyond belief, not without some embellishment I might add, as we were to find out later. However, many were true, as could be seen by the wounds they carried. Dad, for reasons rather unknown, was never called up. Instead he was sent down to the Brush works in Loughborough, where he became a progress manager. One of the projects was the making of Mosquito planes, built entirely of wood which became very successful during the latter part of the war.

However Dad was conscripted in to the A.R.P. which meant duty whenever there was an air raid. Not that Loughborough was attacked, but rather that we were in the path of the Jerry bombing of Coventry, which happened most nights. We lads would spend hours watching the flashes in the sky as the bombs were dropped. One night during a particularly heavy raid over Coventry, Dad was regaled in his white tin helmet, having been promoted to chief in his air-raid shelter. He was standing in the entrance when an unusually heavy explosion occurred. This caused Dad to fall backwards onto the only female member of the shelter. He never actually told me himself about this incident for I believe mother would not have approved of any joke that had ensued from this. Anyway the war eventually ended in 1945. Actually I was in scout camp in the Brecon Beacons in North Wales when peace with Japan was given out.

Some years later I saw the devastation caused by the atom bomb dropped on Hiroshima. The whole city had been flattened and it was an enormous shock to see such destruction. It made me realise that there are no winners from a war. But this was on another voyage in 1951.

Chapter 14

A changing world

The initial part of this book is an oversized essay or whatever has been written purely in the context as I saw my life, partly as I observed it and partly as I let my imagination take me over. It is only when I have re-read everything, that more or less without exception, the majority of it all rings true. Bearing in mind that to date the majority runs from 1945 to 1948, a long time ago and at a most impressionable time in my life. For instance the marvellous invention called the Internet, has allowed me to confirm certain dates and even more information appertaining to the area I am writing about. The biggest surprise to me is how the devil all this information was obtained in the first place.

On telephoning the records office in Kew, I was amazed to find that over six hundred calls were dealt with every day. That for instance in my case although information might be rather sparse reference to the shipping movements at the time and area that I sailed as a cadet, nevertheless a visit to the records office will allow me to research papers which have been kept and recorded for posterity. The amazing thing is that this service, I believe, has been at in existence since 1838. Previously these records were all over the place and much more difficult to authenticate.

Off once more

After only a week at home I was recalled to join the *Lalande* in Liverpool. I could see on my return that discharging of cargo was still continuing. Actually we lads had signed off and signed on the same day before going off, on what we hoped would be more than a week's shore leave. However, I was still a new boy and pleased to get off on another trip. We were to be in the Gladstone dock for a further two weeks during which time I got to know fellow cadets from several other L & H ships doing likewise.

Bearing in mind that the year was 1948 (and I remember it well), the ships in question, were the *Balfe*, *Devis*, and *Murillo*. All company ships were named after painters and artists with one or two exceptions. It is interesting to note what each ship was like. The *Balfe* was of 2000 tonnes and could be mistaken for an ocean tug having been built before the First World War. Going on board was like walking in the past, tiny by comparison with her sister ships, but having served her country well during the war. She was steam driven and with a coal burner and the most ancient of navigation instruments. She also had steering gear from the wheel on the bridge to the steering chains on the main deck. This went to the rudder to steer the ship. All communication was by blowing down pipes as on the *Lalande*. The accommodation was dismal and small and if I remember correctly there were only cold taps. To have a shower you stood on a concrete floor not so good in the northern hemisphere, I can tell you.

As for being in the tropics, a regular run for her, there was no air-conditioning on board and hardly a hot water tap to be seen. Actually, I seem to remember the old man had one. As for lifeboats, well to be honest the Board of Trade, as it was then, (changed the following year to be called the Department of Trade and Industry) made sure that conditions on board merchant ships were improved and then there were big changes afoot. However we all seemed very fond of the *Balfe*.

I suppose she could really go up the back waters in South America, which meant she often took cargoes to places where there was nothing but a local village, straw huts and all that. This meant she became a prime target for people to stowaway on, because of lack of Customs control in the small harbours she visited. Homeward bound she was always stopping at sea to transfer stowaways to a company ship. Outward bound she would return them back to whatever port they had come from.

Only once did this happen to me when I was on the *Murillo*. It meant contacting another company ship that was outward bound, by radio, then hopefully with a reasonable sea, the ships would stop about half a mile from each other, launch a lifeboat and take the luckless stowaways to be returned. Some masters were rather funny about the informality of this procedure and apparently demanded signatures and all sorts before taking them on board. Others were pleased to assist as it often fell to their own company to be in the same predicament and the feeling was soonest forgotten the better for all concerned.

To be quite frank it was the duty of the crew to see that such incidents should not have happened in the first place. I think we should remember that this had been going on for generations. It was one of those things that companies found difficult to control. Providing stowaways were returned, much was overlooked and I believe not always entered in the log. With the war gone and modernisation afoot, changes just had to come about and regulations were vastly enforced.

I well remember Mr Spooner who was still with us waving a hefty bunch of papers in his hand as he passed us on the deck one day and said, "This is your future, lads, paper and more paper, I don't envy you."

Getting back to the *Murillo* the last of the three ships lying alongside in the Gladstone docks, this was to be my next ship after my second trip on the *Lalande*. The *Murillo* was an Empire ship of about 7000 tonnes, a coal burner. All three ships were driven by steam, something I became very attached to. Their massive reciprocating engines, the enormous cylinder heads and crank shafts, pounding night and day stays vividly in my memory.

So it was on the return to Liverpool to join the *Lalande* for my second trip, that a member of staff from head office, The Royal Liver Buildings, was good enough to give up his lunch hour to explain many things about the company. Unlike today the loyalty to staff and the loyalty to the owners were almost paramount. Indeed this did not prohibit a member of the ship's company, which included all disciplines from the ship's master down to the galley boy, from leaving and going elsewhere.

One of the biggest attractions, particularly amongst the single members, was that the more they changed shipping companies the more they would see of the world. As many of the crew members join a ship from the pool, which every port had, then they were only bound to that particular ship until she returned to a home port.

In the case of the cadets, we had little option but to stick as we were either indentured, that is, on a four-year apprenticeship and more or less bound to the company for that period. There was an onus on the company to take heed to our studies. This was mostly done by correspondence course with one of the mates overseeing our progress. In most cases the indentured apprentices had had some short college course to get them started, of which I was one, and during this time approaches were made to various shipping companies.

In the case of cadets these mostly came from either the training ships, *Worcester* or *Conway*. Both were square-rigged ships, lying in estuaries on the coast, and were usually a priority when applying to a shipping company for a berth on the completion of their training.

There were also various other establishments, shore-based such as Warsash, Southampton where I had failed so miserably some sixty years ago.

I was very interested to see, having done my maiden voyage, to note how close knit the company was, both in crews and shore gangs. It had never occurred to me that there might be members of families serving on board the same ship. Twice I met this in my second year and appreciating how confined quarters and working conditions were one could imagine a young first mate with an ageing father as a junior ordinary seaman being together. Not really an ideal situation. This was discussed in somewhat of a jovial mood by us three lads one day on the deck and was overheard by an engineer who firmly put us in our place by informing us how careful the company was towards such problems. He did say however there were a number of Captains with relatives and it had mostly been successful. There were however quite a lot of families in the shore gangs, mostly stevedores, but this wasn't a problem.

Chapter 15

No longer a novice

It is amazing what a five pound a month rise will do to your ego. No big deal I can assure you, but as was explained to us, by a rather harassed clerk from the office, that we should be more grateful. He went on to elaborate by saying, "Do you realise how much it costs to feed you and what is more, you have free accommodation." I am sure that had he not been such a weedy looking character, one of us well might have given him a 'fourpenny one' something rather frowned on today Instead the senior cadet just told him to push off but not quite in those terms as you can imagine.

S.S. Murillo.

The S.S. *Murillo* was an Empire boat, nothing special but what is termed a three-island job. That is, it had a raised bow, midship housing the bridge and main accommodation and stern where the crew and we cadets lived. She was a coal burner and not what you would call particularly handsome.

She was to be my home for however long the company saw fit and like all these appointments you had to put up with it as after all we were all company men. The crew seemed fairly reasonable, but as it turned out, the Bosun, a real old salt in his fifties, or so we guessed, was a Canadian who wore an old vest and a belt back to front. He was always drunk in port and was frequently found lying on the floor, in the galley, which we shared with him. He had fallen off his seat with the balance of his dinner, or whatever, on his face or chest. We lads were forever cleaning him up. To top it all he never took his shoes off for according to him he was always ready for duty and any emergency if he kept them on. This we had to agree with as he was best left alone. Having said that when he was sober he was a brilliant seaman and we learnt a lot from him. It appeared that during the war he was on the Russian convoys and more than once had been in charge of a lifeboat having been torpedoed. That made him a hero in our eyes.

However to jump ahead we were lying in BA in the River Plate, when a directive came from the Board of Trade that all lifeboats were to be lowered regularly to the water to check the gear and their sea worthiness. The Bosun was well aware of the importance of this order having had to use them himself during the war. From then on, thanks to the regulations imposed by the D.T.I., health and safety was tightened up and not before time. Many new ships were coming into line with very stringent regulations.

President Peron, an equivalent to Russia's Stalin was a tyrant who living in BA in total luxury at the end of the Main Avenue with his wife Eva. As you probably know a musical has been made and was been a big hit on the West End stage for many years.

We were informed that all goods marked for Evita Peron were stowed in a lock-up in the hold, this being done under close supervision. When loading and unloading one such case that we had on board there must have been 250 pairs of shoes in it.

Rather a lot it seemed to me when I had only three. It seemed to be a very strict regime and in Buenos Aires very little leeway seemed to be given to their own people of Argentina.

These were also the days of Castro in Cuba and Stalin in Russia, when dictators ruled with a heavy hand, something of which we cadets were advised by the first mate to watch out for ourselves when going ashore. He put sufficient emphasis on things to make sure we got the message. As usual there is always one person who defies these warnings and had it not been for the good offices of the British Consul our junior cadet might have found himself languishing behind bars. Thinking back now we three cadets or should I say two to be correct. There always seemed to be one of us who was missing having found our off duty activities too much to handle.

Up the River Plate

At last with the cargo discharged and lifeboats sorted we proceeded out of North Basin bound upriver for a cargo of grain to be put into the lower hold. I cannot remember exactly but it was to be either No 3 or 4 hatch, the grain would be poured into the hold from the quayside, or from lighters, As you can imagine the air was thick and acrid with grain dust, not really an environment for an asthma suffer. The River Plate, although wide and expansive, is not bottomless like the Amazon. Hence shipping companies like the Royal Mail Line whose run it was had to design ships with shallow draughts allowing them to sail the river with ease.

A similar situation arises in the Maracibo Lakes in Venezuela which was the port for an enormous oil terminal for Shell Mex. The lake being shallow had a fleet of shallow draught tankers of about 3000 tons to transfer oil from the wells to the ocean tankers.

On arriving up river at Zarate and then Rosario, we were informed that we would also be taking meat back in our refrigerators to the UK. This apparently caused much activity from the Argentine authorities as work had to be carried out on the refrigerators to bring us up to standard. As far as I can recollect the *Murillo* had not been on the meat run for some time, so there was a delay of several days whilst work and inspection was carried out. This enabled us cadets to escape ashore and see for ourselves gauchos at work. We lads did our best to get astride a horse for the sheer fun of it, but had very little success I can assure you.

Anyway, the long and the short of it was that the refrigerators were eventually seen fit to carry refrigerated cargo. Now loaded we set out downriver calling at Montevideo and ports north bound. We saw the German battleship, the *Graf Spey* lying off Monty, where she was scuppered by her own German crew. This was rather than be blown to pieces and sunk by the Royal Navy that had pursued her into the South Atlantic in 1942. This was a moment in time that we can only read about now. The bravery of those involved in the Second World War became very apparent to me when I saw this wreck. Part of her super structure was still standing proudly out of the water even then. It must have been an incredible sight to see her going down onto the ocean floor for it is now fifty-five years ago and the sea will have claimed her many years ago.

Our next stop was below Rio loading bails of cotton for the continent and home, wherever that might be, hopefully Liverpool and the prospects of a decent leave. Some two or three weeks later having hedge-hopped up the coast picking up various cargo as we proceeded, the order came to batten down ready for the Continent and UK. Another trip, another experience, but what was I witnessing?

I must try and explain myself without incurring the, "Oh I know" syndrome from the younger generation. It was all very interesting, indeed it was to become fascinating to watch a new world appear and this was only my concept of how things were happening, with communication at a premium. I am only speaking for myself, who up to the present time, didn't even possess a radio and whatever news we did receive from the wireless room was purely referring to shipping weather forecasts and agents' reference to ports to be visited. I must say that on reflection we rarely thought about the outside world, ourselves or our immediate future. This would await us at our next port of entry, hence to a great extent we remained autonomous, or maybe ignorant would be a better way of putting it. Concerned more with the present than the future.

The days of the old tired steam ships in general was starting to close but would be kept going until their replacements could be built to keep the company routes open. This was to be my last but one trip on an old timer. No more belching steam from the engine room, no regular breakdowns and state of the art navigation equipment. Much of it would take time to evolve but it was coming.

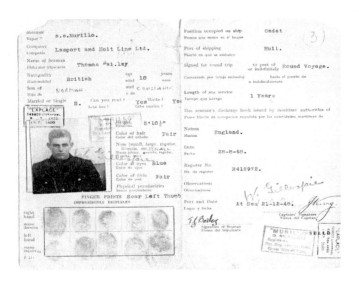

My discharge from the Murillo – Convict?

At last finally loaded we were on our way and we lads were put on day work. We were to leave early morning although no one was prepared to confirm this. The *Murillo* might well be sold to the Greeks not an unusual occurrence then in 1948. One or two ships were coming out of the ship yards to complement the fleet into the Canaries for refuelling.

We saw some of them as we refuelled in Las Palmas with the usual ritual of Priest and Nuns coming for their 'bounty'. Willy Gillespie, our captain being a staunch Catholic was well received. Any ship with Liverpool as its home port sported many Irish amongst its crew.

It is always nice to enter the English Channel, rounding Ushant light on the French coast. Now assigned to the 12-4 watch, I can always remember the 2nd mate saying to me, "We can't come to much harm out here so let's see how you get on." This was to be my first real experience of navigation, rather late in the day, as I had been afloat now for over a year. I was thankful to put into practise the work I had done at the Nautical College in London, reminding myself that in the future when I became 2nd mate I would see that cadets were introduced to the bridge much earlier in their career.

And so I ended another trip. For me it was a time of growing up, a time of learning about my own abilities and indeed my own limitations, of which I was only too aware. The chance to join a fine shipping company as it was, and the security that it gave me was most rewarding and I shall never forget that particular time in my life.

Chapter16

Moving On

After a short leave, I joined the M.V. *Dryden* as senior cadet with all the most up-to-date equipment on board and I was totally new to most of it. We three lads were given time under the guidance of the 2nd mate to acquaint ourselves with the bridge, so at least we were aware of what we were looking at. Everything on board, including the engine room was incredible. However, there was one thing missing and that was the character which especially the *Lalande* had.

With modernisation of equipment, especially on deck, the old hands such as the carpenter and lamp trimmer were no longer required. We were already edging towards a 'throw-away' society. The 'make-do-and-mend' brigade who had dominated my life on the *Lalande*, and to a lesser degree on the *Murillo*, was vanishing. We were now under the auspices of the Board of Trade. To put it bluntly, I as senior cadet and Bill, another cadet who had also come from one of the other old timers, could hardly believe our good fortune having found ourselves aboard such a ship.

The other cadet on his first trip was not as impressed, having obviously been used to the good things in life.

The old man, Captain Griffiths, was a real gent, something very different We had to dress correctly and protocol was expected to be observed, this seemed to come naturally to us all, as he was a very fair man, as I was to find out later. Our other great bonus was our accommodation, situated on the aft end of the boat deck, with sleeping quarters, a day room and bathroom, what a difference this was and at last Bill and I felt that someone 'loved us.'

Fully loaded and down to our fully loaded line we preceded out of the Gladstone dock on high water. Next stop Las Palmas, then round the Cape of Good Hope and on to Fremantle, with approximately thirty-eight days at sea. We had twelve passengers on board. Their names it is impossible to give, but I do remember a young boy with whom we were ordered to play a ball game.

Now with a modern ship and modern equipment, albeit old-fashioned by today's standards, we called into all the main ports. Bypassing Tasmania, we headed for New Zealand and Wellington, known as windy Wellington. We sailed into this magnificent bay surrounded by cliffs. The local newspaper did a story on the Dryden and it was through the editor, who we were helping, that a very welcome invitation came.

By now Xmas was approaching and we were finally discharged. Capt Griffiths, as the old man was called, gave permission for us three to go and accept the invitation. This had come from the editor of the paper to dine with his family on

109

Xmas Day. Having first been given the once-over by the 1st mate before departure, it turned out to be a wonderful day and for those who have never been in New Zealand at Xmas it is lamb and not turkey on the table. They are all wonderful memories.

HAWKE'S BAY
MERCHANT NAVY CLUB.
CLIVE SQUARE,
NAPIER

To Mr Thomas Bailey

Welcome to Napier

The Executive and Members of the Hostesses and Girls Committees extend to you a Cordial Welcome to the Club during your stay in Napier.

A Special Dance is being held in your honour tonight, 16th Jan.

Also Dances every Monday and Friday evening from 8 p.m to 11.30.

On Sundays the Club Rooms are open from 6 p.m. to 10.30 p.m.—Table Tennis, Cards, Games, Bright Music, Sing Songs, etc.—Light Tea and Suppers provided. Posters will be displayed on the ship giving dates of Dances and other Entertainments.

Come along and enjoy yourself
Yours cordially,
PRESIDENT.

After that most unexpected Xmas treat we were ordered to various ports, loading for the UK. I well remember calling in at Napier with Bill and I, having a few hours off. We decided to go for a swim as it was a glorious day and without further adieu ran down to the beach and swam out to a buoy, some half a mile out. This was a rather foolish thing to do without taking some advice about the dangers that might be there.

We were both sitting there on a buoy and enjoying the moment, when a passing boat closed up to us and a shout from the bridge informed us that barracudas had been seen in the bay. The informant might well have been joking, but the situation we found ourselves in caused us some distress. Fortunate for us after a rather harrowing and anxious hour a yacht seeing us came up and kindly took us back to the shore. Apparently we had been taken for something of a ride but who knows? However that was enough for us that afternoon.

Homeward Bound

The next few weeks were spent loading for the UK, and at the end of January 1950 we finally left Adelaide. Now settling down to apparently a successful load and clear of the coast, Bill and I were called to the bridge. I was put on the 8-12 watch and Bill on the 12-4 watch. This was great we were at last practising all we had learnt at our pre-sea colleges.

Every Saturday morning an inspection was done by the old man and the heads of all departments. As senior cadet I tagged along being relieved from the bridge for this duty.

This inspection included accommodation and as we were fortunate to have our own bathroom and as cadets we were required to clean it ourselves. Standing at the rear of this illustrious group and now in our bathroom, I suddenly found that my presence was required by Captain Griffiths. I found the old man with his white gloves off examining the inside of the bath. He turned to me and said, "Feel that, Bailey." I obeyed and he finished by saying, "That will have to be replaced, my lad." I had been horrified to find there was no enamel on the bath. It was obvious to me that the junior cadet had used the wrong cleaner which turned out to be bleach.

I was stunned, especially as I was responsible for whatever the other cadets did. Knowing full well I was in for a rocketing I stood there whilst he berated me by saying, "There is no way you have the money to replace this. I shall therefore stop you a month's wages. Maybe, you will be more careful next time."

It had been a close encounter but I had learnt never to hand work out without checking. That evening I now realised that by the docking of a month's pay, the princely sum of thirteen pounds, I was undecided whether to thump the culprit or give him lots of nasty jobs to do. He was a great guy and had certainly more qualifications, than myself but nevertheless he was the junior. The conclusion I reached was that thirteen pounds from him on pay off would at least sort some thing out. Actually all this came to nothing as you will shortly see.

Crossing the South Pacific and approaching the Cape of Good Hope, South Africa. I was called to the old man's room. Knocking as I entered, I must say I was more than nervous. By this time I was totally jittery thinking I was about to get another telling off reference the bathroom incident, when smiling, broadly he said, "Do you fancy a trip to America, Bailey?" I think by this time, I was totally nonplused. As far as I can remember he repeated this statement and then carried on to say he had a message from Liverpool that I should report to Head Office on my return, as the marine superintendent, Capt. Davis wished to see me. Apparently a message had been received that morning but officially the actual reason for this was to be with held until I reported to the office.

However, and it is only conjecture on my part, I rather feel Captain Griffiths seeing the obvious concern on my face felt he ought to give me some indication saying, "I wouldn't be surprised if you are not going to be promoted." He followed it up by saying, "I have forgotten the bath incident, we can't have a third officer with that on his conscience." I remember going up to him shaking his hand and saying, "I won't let you down sir."

Back home and having presented myself at the office in the Royal Liver Buildings his words were reinforced by my appointment to an American ship the M.V. *Jutahy* which on charter to the company under the Panamanian flag. This was a new departure for me. The one snag was that I had a gap of some weeks as the *Jutahy* was not going to be in New York for a month or two when the change of crew would take place.

It was therefore decided that a further trip on the *Dryden* would do the trick. So after a further run down to South America on the *Dryden* in which time as I was to go on the bridge, I was given wonderful access to all the navigation prior to my promotion as 3rd mate on the *Jutahy*. This was to be another experience, I would never forget. So at the ripe old age of nineteen years I was launched.

This discharge book really helped me to recall my memoirs.

Chapter 17

I join the M.V. Brittanic
New York Bound

LEAVING THE LANDING STAGE at Liverpool. A fine photograph of the Cunard White Star liner *Britannic* moving away from the quayside. This twin-screw vessel has a gross tonnage of 26,943, and was built in 1911 at Belfast by Harland and Wolff. She has a length of 633½ feet, a beam of 82½ feet and a depth of 45½ feet. Her port of registry is Liverpool.

341

If any one had told me that three and a half years after joining the S.S. *Lalande* that filthy night off Greys in the Thames, that I was about to join the *Brittanic*, the last of the White Star line, liners in Liverpool, to travel 1st class to New York, I would never have believed them.

This was however the case and my parents true to form had accompanied me up to Liverpool to see me off. It still didn't stop either of them, offering me lots of advice, on the way up and in a way, I was glad to see the liner, as she lay alongside the pier head in Liverpool.

There had been some confusion about my joining the *Jutahy*, which was supposed to have been in New York already but she had to deviate on the way home from Brazil. I did not know the reason why this was so but only that one way or another it had been sorted out. Consequently in the end, I had only been given a week to get myself ready and as was implied in the office, I might well be away for eighteen months. However the problem was eased as far as I was concerned when a telegram arrived the following day to say that due to delay in the *Jutahy*'s schedule, I would have to wait until the following trip to join her. Would I therefore, rejoin the *Dryden* for one more trip and hopefully, catch up with the *Jutahy* in New York the next time round. In the end it didn't quite work out like that, as there was still a time gap, but I was thrilled to think I was at last on my way again.

On the positive side, this allowed Dad, who was a tailor, time to make me a suit for which I was very grateful. Unfortunately it was such an outdated style. Still it was the thought that counted. I never wore it, as it was totally out of fashion, so thanking Dad profusely I packed it at the bottom of my trunk and forgot about it.

So the beginning of July 1950 saw me standing on the landing stage opposite the Royal Liver buildings in Liverpool, saying goodbye to my parents. We had driven that morning up from Loughborough. I shall never forget the view over Derbyshire before we arrived at our destination. I think I was so excited about going to New York as a passenger that everything looked very special and vivid to me.

The *Britannic* lay alongside, in the river, opposite the Royal Liver Buildings. A little after midday I said my goodbyes to my parents, who like many others were determined to stay and see the ship's departure. As we were all first class passengers, everything was taken care of, no carrying suitcases this time.

Eventually I was accompanied to our cabin. I say ours as there were two of us, the other person as yet I had not met. He turned out to be an American gentleman who was going out on business.

You must remember this that even after the war and in the early '50s most passengers, were either going home on business, or wealthy people who may be travelling the world. But the real tourist trade as we know it today was still on a very small scale.

The *Britannic* had a capacity for 140 passengers. Her twin the *Georgic* had burnt out in the Suez Canal. Those who are old enough will remember the Suez Crisis when Anthony Eden was Prime Minister and that part of the world was very unstable.

With all the goodbyes and waving of hands to our friends on the quayside and tugs fast, we moved slowly into the river. It was very pleasant indeed to be underway in a first-class liner as a passenger with everything you required.

Having settled in, I spent some time wandering round the decks. Luckily time was passing along most pleasantly. The evening meal was at 7pm, which I was pleased about as I was feeling the pangs of hunger setting in. I was to be at a table for four.

I was joined at the table by two Americans who totally ignored me during their meal. I felt very uncomfortable so I eased the situation, by excusing myself as soon as I could. I made a somewhat hasty retreat and I was glad to get away. I only hoped that the one absent member of our table, whoever it might be would appear in the morning and things might be easier.

The following morning, after a somewhat fitful sleep as I was a little nervous sharing a cabin with a complete stranger (actually during the voyage he became a good friend and a very interesting one at that), I ventured down to breakfast to note that I was the only one present at our table. No doubt the others were having a lie in. I was just contemplating the menu, when I noticed the chair next to me being moved. "Good morning," said a very American female voice. "How are you this morning, young man?" I looked up, to see one of the most colourful characters imaginable about to sit down next to me.

With a delightful smile she said, "And what is your name, young man?" Being a little nonplussed by this, I believe, I replied, "Jim Bailey," in reply to which, she said, "I shall call you James. My name is Mrs Fred Helman, but you just call me Ma'am for short."

I just have to describe Ma'am. She was less than five feet tall, very Jewish looking with a black and gold cap on her head, a wonderful gold and black dress to the floor and tiny black and gold slippers with turned-up toes. She was to me an elderly lady, possibly in her eighties, glasses hung round her neck on a gold chain and to cap it all, an enormous cigarette holder. I never saw her without it and it always had a lighted cigarette in it, even during meals.

Having taken a mouth of food she would keep the smoking going – rather reminiscent of the 1920's films I had seen. The rings on her fingers were something else, not that I know anything about rings but as the Yanks would say "this was some loaded babe" or maybe "chick" depending on where they hailed from.

It soon became plain to me that although we all spoke the same language, albeit often spelt rather differently, that the American humour and general demeanour would take a little working out.

I was thrilled to have such an affable character sitting next to me as earlier on I had wondered whether I wouldn't have rather stayed at home. It was quickly very obvious to me, that Ma'am intended to show me the way of the Americans and immediately enquiring, if I had ordered my breakfast, I shook my head, then she said, "You're going to have ham and eggs, Virginia ham and eggs of course."

By this time a waiter was hovering over Ma'am. This I noticed was the case throughout the seven days we were on board and was soon to realise, that this lady was a well-seasoned traveller.

Madam's husband, or to be correct, Mrs Fred Helman's husband had been President of the "Bank of California" and as such, seemed to have privileges way beyond anything I had ever known before. Mrs Hellman had travelled the world extensively and as time and money were of no consequence to her she seemed to spend much of her time (or rather had, as she must be well in her 80s and seemingly, slowing down) meeting important people. One was General Smuts, the famous South African, whom she waxed lyrically about.

By this time our breakfasts had arrived, my new companion had berated the steward for the lack of eggs on my plate. Anyway rather than appear to be unappreciative of her attention, I went along with it, not knowing really what else to do.

One of the Cunard White Star Line Menu covers.

Luncheon

Tomato Juice   Clam Juice

HORS D'ŒUVRE

Bismarck Herrings   Petits Oignons   Salade Niçoise   Choux-fleurs
Cornichons   Anchovies in Oil   Sardines   Smoked Salmon
Salade Russe   Egg Aurore   Tomato Windsor

Saucisson : Lyon, Liver and Cervalet   Olives : Queen and Farçie

SOUPS

Consommé Diablotins .   Potage Soissonaise

FISH

Fillet of Hake, Portugaise   Cold : Fresh Lobster, Mayonnaise

FARINACEOUS

Gnokis Sicilienne

VEGETARIAN

Egg in Cocotte, Jeannette

ENTREES

Fried Calf's Liver, Fines Herbes   Savoury Lamb and Vegetable Stew

AMERICAN SPECIALITY

Creamed Minced Chicken on Waffle

JOINT

Roast Prime Ribs of Beef, Horseradish Cream

VEGETABLES

String Beans   Leaf Spinach   New Carrots

POTATOES

Baked Jacket, Mashed, Sautées and French Fried

GRILL (To order 10 minutes)

Sirloin Steak, Maître d'Hôtel
Jumbo Squab, Straw Potatoes

COLD BUFFET

Roast Lamb   Roast Beef   Roast Duckling   Ox Tongue
Galantine of Capon   Roast Turkey   Leicester Brawn   York Ham

SALADS

Lettuce   Tomato   Mixed Bowl   Augustin   Fresh Fruit

DRESSINGS

Ritz   Thousand Island   French

SWEETS

Sago Custard   Gateau au Chocolat   Rhubarb Pie
Compôte of Peaches, Cherries and Pineapple, Whipped Cream

ICES

Vanilla   Raspberry   Banana

CHEESES

Stilton   Kraft   Port Salut   Edam   Gorgonzola   Cheshire
Philadelphia Cream   Roquefort   Gruyere   Camembert   Blue

Tea   Fresh Fruit   Coffee

Passengers on Special Diet are especially invited to make known their
requirements to the Head Waiter
Specialty Foods for Infants are available on request.

During those seven days all four of us generally got along well thanks to various interventions from Ma'am and during that time, we explored the ship, with its libraries, cocktail bars, quiet rooms and restaurants.

Ma'am, obviously due to her age, always retired in the afternoon and appeared just short of the evening meal which was always a hoot. The old girl had a wonderful sense of humour and the stewards rose to this so there were always little quips here and there.

I was fortunate enough to have a little look at the bridge along with other passengers one morning. Although it was an old ship, about twenty years old by this time, I have to say the set up was incredible. The Cunard White Star Line certainly knew their business in shipping.

The evening before we were due to arrive in New York, we were having a night cap in the bar, when Ma'am suddenly said to me, "I want you to come along to my cabin tomorrow night, James, as it will be the last chance I have to show you something, I think you might be interested in."

So the following evening after a very convivial meal all of us by this time were getting on fine and Ma'am had provided champagne for our table. Mam suddenly left the table cigarette and holder on full power and turning to me, she said, "See you shortly, young man." I had been given my instructions how to find Ma'am's cabin, as she explained, it is just under the Captain's quarters. This meant I had to leave my lowly, but very nice cabin amidships, for the upper deck.

It was often the case on liners such as this, that the name of the occupant was inserted in a brass holder on the side of, as in this case, the suite door.

At last I found it and very tentatively knocked, having done a rapid change of clothes before going along there. The door opened almost immediately and there stood a black servant in maid's uniform, "Please come in," she gestured me into the room, which was enormous and then, through into an equally big room where Ma'am was sitting on a sofa.

The maid introduced us formally with Ma'am brushing her aside at the same time, saying, "Come and sit down, James, what will you have to drink?"

We chatted about the voyage. She went on a little about the maid saying it was not easy to get decent servants these days, but it was all very pleasant I must say.

A couple of highballs later, she stood up and asked me to follow her. It appeared we were entering the bedroom, as there was a large bed in it. She beckoned me towards the bed. "What do you think about those, James?" she said. On the bed laid out, were the most incredible, and I would have imagined the most expensive garments I had ever seen and remain so to this day. Rather like the clothes she wore all the time but obviously far more luxurious, consisting of cap, dress, shoes, the lot all in gold lamé. "These are the clothes I shall wear, when the time comes." It dawned on me that these would be the clothes she would be buried in.

Slowly we walked back into the other room and had a nightcap, we were due into New York in the early hours of the morning. It would be most unlikely if I would see her again. We said our goodbyes, and for me it had been an extraordinary week with my encounter with Mrs Fred Hellman the icing on the cake.

I went on deck to see the lights of ships converging on the city of New York. It had all been a great experience and with New York our destination in the morning, I felt as if a new chapter was starting in my life.

Chapter 18

New York July 1950

After a wonderful seven days on the M.V. *Britannic* and then to step ashore in New York this was something else. I had been given the briefest of details of how to get to the Lamport & Holt's office in Brookland. Once off the ship and standing on the quayside, with the mandatory seaman's trunk, which housed my entire belongings, I suddenly felt more than isolated from the rest of the world.

To add to this, the priority was being given by the cab drivers to those passengers who obviously could give the big tips. I certainly didn't fall into that category. Eventually after a good half hour's wait I was on my way and within a short time found myself inside the company offices.

I think the interesting thing about all this is our perception of how we see things. To walk into the head office in Liverpool with all its grandeur and history, and magnificent models of ships of days gone by, was awe inspiring. Then it all becomes a shock, when you walk into a paper-strewn office which is purely a work place with nothing very grand about it. The whole place was very laid back, everyone had rolled up sleeves and an air of "What do you want?"

After introducing myself to the one whom I assumed to be in charge I waited for some acknowledgement. Whilst he still carried on flicking through his papers in front of him, he eventually addressed me. Without any sort of introduction he informed me, so the whole office could hear that the *Jutahy* was still at sea and seemed at a loss what to do with me.

I must say the manager, (who I am glad to say was British, a rather unusual term to day) had luckily got out of bed on the right side that morning and, seeing my concern, sorted things out. Before long I was on my way to the officers' club in Times Square, where I was to stay until the arrival of the *Jutahy*. A tune came out of the cabbie radio, one I remember to this day and it was "Come on along and listen to a lullaby of Broadway". It is amazing how a brief recall can bring back so many memories. It is so unlike today when we all know so much about the world through television even if you have never been there. But for me it was that I was observing a whole new world, untainted by any preconceived ideas without a doubt.

The hustle and bustle of New York was something I had never experienced before even though I had spent several months in London at Sir John Cass and Roland House. The armed police and the high buildings totally overwhelmed me. By the time the cabby had pulled up in Times Square, a rather exhausted 19-year-old was more than glad to have arrived at his destination. By sheer luck, at least as far as I was concerned, he stopped immediately outside the entrance to the officers' club. I stood on the sidewalk (note the Americanism creeping in) petrified, to be absolutely honest, as to whom I was going to meet when I stepped inside. However I remembered the old saying always be polite and stand when a lady comes into the room. Something our grandchildren laugh about when I go on a bit today about the lack off manners etc.

Anyway the accommodation was not too bad but like all subordinates I was given a back and often not entirely wholesome room. Without question the view was of washing and brick walls so I suppose it could have been any city in the world. However, after a couple of days, the office got in touch with me, to say that my ship the M.V. *Jutahy*, would be docking in Hoboken the following afternoon.

True to form, I found myself the following afternoon standing at the bottom of the gangway of the *Jutahy*. She was already discharging her cargo and, leaving my trunk on the quayside, I strode up the gangway.

Before proceeding any further I should state that many ships were taken into service at the end of the war to supplement those that had befallen Hitler's U-boats. The *Jutahy* was a new addition to the company's fleet and very possibly on charter from another company. To be honest with you I don't really know, but she did carry the Panamanian flag.

What I do know is that she was ideal for the run up rivers etc, especially the Amazon which she was designed for with air-conditioning and ice-cold drinking water. How different to the old *Lalande*.

The M.V. Jutahy

Small and shallow of draught she was perfect for the job with a crew of only 16. She was economical and she was American built with the latest equipment much of which I had read about but certainly was unfamiliar with. I was looking forward to getting to sea. However we were to be alongside for the next ten days, discharging and loading.

My first job I had to do was to familiarize myself with everything on board. This I did in conjunction with the 1st Mate, Michael Bennett who was one of the boys, a great guy, which I supposed you had to be, if you were stuck out away from home as many merchant seamen were for such long periods of time.

I join the M.V. Jutahy Aug 1950

The first thing that struck me was how well equipped she really was, to go to one of the warmest spots with temperatures up to one hundred and twenty degrees Fahrenheit and ninety degrees humidity. It would make such a difference to crew comforts with such things as iced water and air-conditioning. This was something new indeed and a far cry from the *Lalande*.

There must have been hard days in the seafaring days of yesteryear. But I suppose what you hadn't had you never missed, a far cry from today. To coin a phrase it must have been hell before the turn of the century on the trade ships sailing the world.

Well ensconced and with all the latest equipment on board, although unfamiliar to me, I was anxious to get to sea to see how everything worked.

We spent the next ten days discharging and loading, with most evenings spent ashore. Apparently the first mate was getting somewhat entangled with one of the females in a nearby bar with her father the bar owner. He was keen to see their relationship maturing. As I was on my first trip and unaware of the 'goings on' I found the whole affair intriguing. I was told this had been going on for the last year with the *Jutahy* coming into Hoboken, the port for New York, every six weeks.

As we always used the same berth in Hoboken and our trips down to Brazil were of a regular six weeks' duration. Romona, that was her name was getting very attached to Michael the 1st mate. Her father managed to somehow or other obtain a blood sample from Michael possibly when he was well intoxicated, in the hope that progress could be made, as it was mandatory then to have a blood sample before a marriage could go ahead. What lengths fathers will go to for their daughters!

I have to say that it was not long before Michael, with a little advice from those who could see what was going to happen, managed to extricate himself from this unfortunate situation. Apparently the office had got wind of this and was glad sanity had prevailed.

Jim Bailey on the left – non commissioned 3rd officer with Michael Bennett.

The old man Capt Casey had arrived back, after a week and things seemed to hot up, as they say. Eventually, late one night with the *Jutahy* well battened down, we slipped our moorings and slid out into the open water and with New York astern we headed out for the Nantucket light vessel and the open sea.

Bearings were taken of points ashore to ascertain our position and the old man had half an hour on the bridge with me, just to make sure I knew my duties then left the bridge, with strict orders to call him at any time should his expertise be needed. I was ecstatic and having checked the helmsman's course I went out on to the wing of the bridge. The lights of New Jersey were just coming up as dusk settled in. I remember it as if it was yesterday. I thought of Mum and Dad and wished them goodnight. It had been a full and exciting day.

What a fantastic sight it had been, leaving New York and what an experience it had been. Now, with the pilot away and full ahead rung down to the engine room, it was my watch and vigilance was the order of the day.

The old man had hardly spoken to me, only enough really to confirm that I was the "3rd mate James Bailey" that the company had sent to join the ship. The old man was very short on words so it was not really the best way to start a relationship. But that was nothing unusual in those days to be kept at arm's length.

Many is the time I had to take solace with either the 1st or 2nd mate referring to this apparent gulf between Captain Casey and myself. Later when I got to know him he wasn't a bad old stick but very introverted and single-minded when it came to the running of his ship.

It is now I feel the appropriate moment to unveil to you the crew on the *Jutahy*, very different, I can assure you to those I had sailed with up to that moment in time. We three Mates were British. The Chief Steward was from Liverpool. The three Engineers were German and all had served in U-boats. The Chief was from Liverpool and I could see he was near retirement. The Wireless Operator was Polish and the rest of the crew were all from South America with Portuguese, as their everyday language.

Getting to sea after days in port when the ship is working all hours often in filthy condition is not so inspiring. But then to come on the bridge the following morning to see the whole ship washed down and everything stowed away with just the gentle dipping of the bow into a clear sea and sky is I think one of those magical moments. It is a feeling of thank goodness normality has set in. With ten days or a fortnight of peace and, with luck, a good passage we should be well on our way.

Our first port of call was to be Port of Spain Trinidad. It so happened that during the war a student from that country studying at Loughborough College, was billeted on us. If I could only have remembered his name and address, I could well have had a free meal. Ah well we can all have dreams!

I was only just realising that I was no longer a cadet, albeit a non commissioned 3rd mate with a lot to learn. Nevertheless it was just dawning on me, that there would be no more washing down, no more painting or splicing wires. Still I could say I had done it all which seemed to something the American officers I had met ashore had not done. They seemed to come almost direct from nautical schools onto the bridge. Certainly my grounding on the dear old *Lalande*, would stand me in good stead for the future.

It was only after a day or so out that I realised we had passengers on board. In fact there were four of them. A man wearing a dog collar, obviously a minister of whatever religion, his wife and what was most surprising two very young children.

Not as yet being party to all that was going on I was somewhat surprised to see them sitting below on the old man's deck. However all became clear to me when the following morning after sights had been taken, the old man asked me, as it was my watch, if I could cope with a passenger on the bridge for a look around.

Naturally I said yes and within the hour the Vicar appeared on the bridge. I was quite taken back by this, but after the usual courtesies showed him around to the best of my ability as I still had much to learn myself. Apparently he was going to a living somewhere in Brazil but quite where I had yet to find out.

He said that as flights were so few and far between and as he had his wife and two young children with him, by boat might be the best way to travel. Somehow or other he had persuaded the office in New York to allow him passage and after consultation with the Old man and Chief Steward they were allowed to come on board as passengers.

Quite where they were actually going we were not party to and, as we were not blessed with much room in the saloon, the family ate separately and by and large seemed very content with the arrangements.

Actually on leaving the bridge, he did ask me if he could be of any assistance to me. I discovered he had offered this help to others on board. Whether this was religious or not and he was trying to save our souls I never did find out.

Can you spot 'Tuppy' and yours truly on the left – note the Panamanian Flag

I was blessed with a steward by the name of Tuppy, who looked after us three mates. He was a tiny man by any standards with a good head of hair and a black moustache, well known so I was told for his prowess with the ladies.

All went well on board, food was good and the general ambience the best I had ever encountered in my previous three years.

At the end of the first week now feeling more at home we were parallel with the West Indies, when an unfortunate state of events happened in the engine room. One of the big generators had packed up, which was affecting the work of the engine room.

The Chief Engineer asked for a stop which in the end took most of 24 hours. The engine room staff were quite happy to work straight through, but asked for cases of beer to be sent down. After all it was 150 degrees on the plates.

My job when not on watch duty was to liaise with the Chief Engineer and then inform the old man of any progress that was being made. Suffice it to say the engine room lads did a wonderful job and the next morning saw us underway with the generator repaired.

During the night however, I did my duty and liaised as required and on visiting the Chief in his cabin observed him breathing very heavily with an asthma attack. I tried to help the old feller who must have been in his late 50s.

On hearing he had run out of his inhaler I went to my cabin, being an asthma sufferer myself and on handing the spray to him on my return he stood to thank me but dropped the glass spray and then stepped on it, trying to pick it up. Luckily, I had a spare one but you can guess the scene yourselves. It is funny how incidents from years ago stick in your mind.

Later that week we arrived in Trinidad, but for only an overnight alongside, progressing then south, across the mouth of the Amazon then across the Equator and down to Bahia where the final cargo was unloaded.

This was all old territory now, a couple of the company ships were in port. One was the *Balfe* where I learnt the sad news that a good chum of mine, who had been a cadet with me had drowned in Santos harbour. It seemed he just went missing and was found later between the harbour wall and another ship.

I was devastated as Barry had been a very good friend. Maybe or more than likely, was that he had missed his footing having had a few drinks and slipped. Surprisingly he could not swim. His father was a trawler skipper and Barry had done many trips out into the North Sea with him in school holidays. What a sadness it must have been for his family.

Thinking back, I have to say that there were no requirements for those on the high seas to be able to swim. However when you think about it a few strokes would not keep you afloat if your ship went down in the ocean. If you were unlucky enough to find yourself without help at hand or lifesaving equipment to keep you afloat long enough to be picked up by a lifeboat or whatever, then possibly a hasty end might be the best option.

One morning whilst on route down to Bahia the Reverend had popped his head round the door into the chart room, with a request that he might look where we were. It was nice to see him and to introduce him to the chart and our present position. He then turned to me looking some what baffled, "When will we be going into the Amazon?" he exclaimed. "I thought that was where we were heading?"

He had made a most remarkable statement as we were going to Bahia to finally discharge. Straitening up and looking at me, he repeated. "I thought that was where we were going?" I told him that I could not really pinpoint where we were to go, whereupon he started to tell me a most interesting story. He and his family were en route to a missionary station in the northern part of the River Amazon. With so few flights to this part of the world, he had taken the chance to go by sea, in the hope that a way could be found to get him to his destination.

How he intended to do this, with a very young family, the mind boggles. To start off we had no orders ourselves to go up the Amazon and how he expected to do this was way beyond me. After some thought, I decided I should tell the old man about this. I should have realised he would already know!

I think to be fair, the old man knew the situation with regard to the position the company had put him in and on the assumption that there were always ships going up the river. There was always a possibility that this could be sorted out or as a last resort they could be put ashore to wait for some other means of transportation.

In what was a hostile environment, nothing but hot weather and little or no places to drop them off and a responsibility for their lives on board his ship, it was no wonder the Reverend reacted as he did.

However by sheer luck our orders after final discharge were to go to Belem (Para) in the mouth of the Amazon and thence up to Manaus 1000 miles upriver. The ingenuity which our vicar showed, on being advised that we would be going in the direction in which he wished to go, was astounding. For when we arrived in Belem it seemed like fate as everything seemed to be organised with regards to the requirements of our intrepid vicar and his family.

Whether by persuasion or by any other means he had made arrangements to go so far with us I never knew, but we would put the missionary family ashore and from then they would go on by mule.

It was then and only then, that a snippet of news came our way. The reason for the Reverend doing all this was to replace a missionary from the heart of the Brazilian jungle who had been killed by a pygmy arrow.

All we did know was that the Reverend and family were going to face a tough time travelling for many days to reach their destination.

This apparently had all been ratified in the office before the old man would go any further. So, several days later after a very uneventful run, some 600 miles up the river, in the early morning light, the *Jutahy* pulled into a clearing, tying up to the roots of trees.

We had been advised before leaving Belem, that handlers were awaiting our arrival which was some help. What we did not know until much later was that the mules and handlers had been there weeks waiting for us. We were fairly confident of finding a clearing, similar to the one I had encountered on my first trip on the *Lalande*.

A ship that had docked ahead of us in Belem before we left was able to say that they had observed men and mules encamped, obviously awaiting our arrival.

How on earth all this information had been received I have no idea, but we must remember, that time was not of the essence, I believe however that someone in Manaus further up the river, had liaised with Belem.

Possibly all this information had come down from local craft plying the river. After putting a lifeboat over the side, which was the only safe way to get the Reverend and his young family ashore safely, the bosun made a short observation of the bank and was able to discharge his valuable cargo. As far as I can remember they were met by half a dozen mules and their handlers who were pygmy Indians.

The last we saw of them, the family were astride the mules being lead by the indigenous Indians and within minutes they vanished into the jungle. The pack mules brought up the rear and I know we wished them all the luck in the world for we never saw them again.

Days later our uncommunicative old man made the statement to me on watch that he wondered if they would survive. I think in a way he could have relaxed more with all of us but that was how it was.

We heard on the following trip that they had travelled a long way before reaching this outlandish mission. Once again we all wished them God speed. You couldn't do otherwise as there was little or no contact with the outside world, no medical team and certainly no mobile phones. I have often wondered what would have been their fate. I put this last venture down as one of the most memorable of that trip.

With the family away we continued upriver to Manaus, on the way passing on the port side the famous River Negro. I believe years later the actor Michael Bentine's son was lost in this region. I heard on the News that his father went to look for him but he must have been lost up one of the tributaries of the Amazon. This is a wild and desolate place where dugout canoes abound and every thing that is native is real life.

A regular Amazon scene.

The many dugouts we encountered on our way up this mighty river, alligators on the shore, sleeping, and natives in their dugouts spearing fish, is an everyday sight. For the biggest thrill you only had to sound the ship's siren and the sky would be full of the most exotic birds of every kind and colour. Sleeping alligators would slide down the banks into the river and the air was full of shrieks from the jungle.

I will never ever forget.

For the present however we were approaching Manaus. It seemed impossible to me that such a place could exist so far from anywhere

That morning we lay off the quay, ready to go alongside. There it was, a busy thriving native town. However, for details I will have to refer to books.

I certainly can't remember everything and there was little time to go ashore. Loading, as we were, and apparently running late we were required back at Belem as soon as possible.

It would only take us three days to get back to Belem as indeed it would have taken us the best part of six days to come direct from Belem to here. That shows you the strength of the current coming down from the Andes.

However, one thing comes to mind that is that Manaus boasts an opera house, and curiosity getting the better of me I was determined to see this apparent jewel of the Amazon.

The Opera House

Having a couple of hours to spare before final loading, I went ashore and by sheer luck hit upon this magnificent building. It was only reading a book on Brazil lately that I saw this picture and it all came back to me. This magnificent building was built by the rubber companies in the early part of the 19th century, it was taken out to Manaus having been designed and I believe first assembled possibly in England.

The Opera House at Manaus.

Having little time to spare and seeing a side door, I like a naughty boy went in to find myself just in front of the stage. Not daring to ponder, I looked round the auditorium to see this magnificent theatre with its boxes and tiers.

Years later when I went to see Agatha Christie's *The Mouse Trap* in London at the Ambassadors I realised it was almost identical.

From then on we did several trips up the Amazon, each one breathtaking, but from what I hear on the television and read in the newspapers great swathes of the jungle have been cleared and turned into a wilderness. I had been very fortunate to have enjoyed it as it was. So much destruction has taken place in the fifty-five years since I ventured up there.

Fifteen months later I did my last trip in the *Jutahy* returning to New York and thence home to Sir John Cass Nautical College in London to prepare for my 2nd mate's certificates. I have to admit I had not done much studying whilst I had been on board so wondered how I would fare.

137

On arriving back in New York, there was a letter from Dad advising me that Tommy Love, a boat club friend of his, was staying at the George Hotel on 42nd Street. He was hanging bells cast in Taylor's Bell foundry in Loughborough and would love to see me.

We were paid off in New York in dollars at the rate of four to the pound, rather different to today! As we had been away for over a year, I received 700 dollars, which I guarded with my life, or so I thought.

Anyway, I contacted Tommy Love having got off the subway train at Grand Central Station and phoned him at the George. Within half an hour, having hailed a taxi, I was standing outside this very hotel. I went to pay the cabby and finding no wallet in my pocket I leave the next five minutes to your imagination! I realised it wasn't on my person, it had not fallen into the cab and neither had it fallen on to the sidewalk.

There was only one answer and that I had stupidly left it back in the subway when I had phoned Tommy. By this time I was almost delirious and giving the cabby my precious Rolex oyster watch as security he kindly took me back to the underground station.

I don't believe what happened to this day. As I hurtled round the security barrier with an attendant in hot pursuit. I passed probably ten phone boxes to where I thought I had phoned from, then there before my eyes was my wallet – open but with nothing missing. I sallied forth, thanking the Good Lord for a fortuitous ending. How on earth someone passing had not seen my wallet, I shall never know.

Suffice it say, I cleared my self with the security chap and glad I was to see the cabby still there. I gave him a ten dollar tip and retrieved my watch and strolled up towards 42nd Street, wondering what next was in store for yours truly.

I spent the next couple of days with Tommy and a friend of his Sam. We had a good meal out and I am afraid to say somewhat the worst for drink which, believe it or not, I had as yet not had too much debauchery. Still as the saying goes 'there is always a first time'.

However I did have time to go to Greenwich Village to listen to the Jazz and buy a new sports jacket with the shops open all night. I felt very lucky to have redeemed my wallet.

Don't I scrub up well.
Photo taken in Greenwich Village about 3a.m.

The end of the week saw the *Jutahy* outward bound for Baltimore, and then off to the West Indies. It had been quite a wrench leaving, as it had been a great adventure. However now was the time for me to return to the U.K. The crew on the *Jutahy* had been just one big happy family and a hoot from morning to night. I don't think I ever saw such camaraderie on a ship quite like that again. Perhaps it was the extraordinary mixture of nationalities and that we all gelled so well together. It was to keep me in good stead later on.

The end of the week saw my departure. Having said goodbye to the office, I joined the United States cargo ship the *American Chieftain*, lying in Hoboken, bound for Liverpool.

It had been my intention if I could manage it, to hopefully gain some experience which could only help my studies on my return to Sir John Cass.

Chapter 19

The American Chieftain

Next morning, having cleared the coast and with a good breakfast inside me, I knocked on the Captain's day room, to enquire if I might go on the bridge. With a welcome "Come in" I entered.

"What can I do for you?" he said seeing me just as a passenger, which of course I was. Standing up and shaking my hand, I explained to him my position and that I was going back to take my 2nd mates certificate.

"Well," he said looking me up and down, for after all I was a passenger, "what can I do for you, young man?" So with both barrels loaded, I blurted out, "Would it be possible for me to observe a bridge watch, Sir?" The old man seemed quite tickled by this and looking me up and down, said he would have a word with his officers. He beckoned me to sit down and asked me all about myself. A couple of days later I was to go up on the 8 to 12 watch.

So, armed with my sextant, log book and all my own gear, I climbed the steps to the bridge. I will never forget entering the wheel house and introducing myself. After all this was 1950 and after having been in British ships this American ship was much more modernised. Nevertheless it seemed very different, there were chuckles all round. "What the hell have you brought those things for!" the 3rd officer exclaimed, "We navigate different to that here," he said in a southern drawl.

So I learnt the American way of navigating, using the latest navigational aids. It wasn't so different really but was just more modern and up-to-date, than I had been used to. I spent many happy days learning the ways of my friends. There was however a startling difference between the training we received on a British ship and an American ship.

The American Chieftain.

Basically we spent the best part of four years what was called in the days of sail 'before the mast'. In other words we learnt a trade from the engine room to the bridge usually either going to a nautical college, or a training ship, such as the *Conway* or *Worcester*. These were run on naval lines where every kind of seamanship was learnt.

As dear old Captain King once said to me, "Never ask anyone to do anything you cannot do yourself."

The final saga came a day or two later, when a fellow passenger asked me if I would mind swapping my cabin for his as I had a double room. I had noticed his interest in a lady passenger and with nothing more than a nod and a wink we had changed cabins (lucky chap!).

So home at last

After a very pleasant couple of weeks, where we visited the family, Dad insisted I wore my uniform, no big deal as far as I was concerned, but it made him happy. Then up to Sir John Cass (Nautical College), for some revision, I managed to acquire a bed at Roland House once again, which was looking rather the worse for wear, However Ma had gone and it wasn't the same. It could never be the same, there was only one Ma.

All my pals had gone too, nevertheless, it sufficed. With a lot of hard work and with a certain amount of trepidation, I sat and past my 2nd mates exam! It had all been worth it after all.

A Final Thought.

Well, folks, that about wraps it up. At least I have written down the experiences I had during those early almost immature days up to the ripe old age of twenty-one years. Well, I was almost twenty-one, not quite, however as I still had a few months to go. Then I would be lucky enough to be with my parents on that very special day, when I was to be presented with my Rolex Oyster wrist watch by mother.

Anticipating that I would be on the high seas on my actual birthday, I received the watch prior to joining the *Jutahy*, in New York, it was just as well that I had managed to retrieve it after my unfortunate escapade in New York. In actual fact, I think, mother was a little sceptical about it all, however, I decided to tell them, whether or not they believed me or not, it is doubtful as I must say it all seemed rather far-fetched, even to me, sitting as we were, at home in the dinning room.

Dad poured us a small sherry to celebrate, the occasion. To the best of my knowledge the sherry had been in the dining room cupboard all during the war and tasted somewhat weak. Which was no doubt due to my occasional snifter, so to speak, when I replaced the amount I had drunk by toping the bottle up from the cold water tap to escape the inevitable telling off.

They were great days, now looking back the old saying, "Boys will be Boys" is very apt.

It is only on reviewing the book several times and taking onboard the title *Changing Times* that it has dawned on me why I have written about this particular time in my life. There would be many oceans to cross in the future and many continents to visit each one leaving memories indelibly imprinted on my mind. But it was that first trip that made the most impression on me and was, I believe the steepest learning curve in my life.